Knowing God's Will
NKJV

Proverbs 16:9

A man's heart plans his way,
But the LORD directs his steps.

Proverbs 16:9

Knowing God's Will
NKJV

Proverbs 3:5-7

Trust in the LORD with all your heart,
And lean not on your own understanding;
In all your ways acknowledge Him,
And He shall direct your paths.
Do not be wise in your own eyes;
Fear the LORD and depart from evil.

Proverbs 3:5-7

Knowing God's Will
NKJV

Jeremiah 29:11-13

I know the thoughts that I think toward you, says the LORD, thoughts of peace and not of evil, to give you a future and a hope. Then you will call upon Me and go and pray to Me, and I will listen to you. And you will seek Me and find Me, when you search for Me with all your heart.

Jeremiah 29:11-13

Knowing God's Will
NKJV

Romans 12:2

Do not be conformed to this world, but be transformed by the renewing of your mind, that you may prove what is that good and acceptable and perfect will of God.

Romans 12:2

Knowing God's Will
NKJV

Isaiah 30:21

Your ears shall hear a word behind you,
saying,
"This is the way, walk in it,"
Whenever you turn to the right hand
Or whenever you turn to the left.

Isaiah 30:21

Knowing God's Will
NKJV

1 John 5:14-15

This is the confidence that we have in Him, that if we ask anything according to His will, He hears us. And if we know that He hears us, whatever we ask, we know that we have the petitions that we have asked of Him.

1 John 5:14-15

Self-Image
NKJV

Psalm 139:13-14

You formed my inward parts;
You covered me in my mother's womb.
I will praise You, for I am fearfully and
wonderfully made.

Psalm 139:13-14

Self-Image
NKJV

1 Samuel 16:7

The LORD does not see as man sees; for man looks at the outward appearance, but the LORD looks at the heart.

1 Samuel 16:7

W9-AHH-778

Self-Image
NKJV

Jeremiah 9:23-24

Thus says the LORD:
"Let not the wise man glory in his wisdom,
Let not the mighty man glory in his might,
Nor let the rich man glory in his riches;
But let him who glories glory in this,
That he understands and knows Me."

Jeremiah 9:23-24

Self-Image
NKJV

Philippians 2:3-5

Let nothing be done through selfish ambition or conceit, but in lowliness of mind let each esteem others better than himself. Let each of you look out not only for his own interests, but also for the interests of others. Let this mind be in you which was also in Christ Jesus.

Philippians 2:3-5

Knowing God's Will
NASB

Proverbs 3:5-7

Trust in the LORD with all your heart
    And do not lean on your own understanding.
In all your ways acknowledge Him,
    And He will make your paths straight.
Do not be wise in your own eyes;
    Fear the LORD and turn away from evil.

                        Proverbs 3:5-7

Knowing God's Will
NASB

Proverbs 16:9

The mind of man plans his way,
    But the LORD directs his steps.

                        Proverbs 16:9

Knowing God's Will
NASB

Romans 12:2

Do not be conformed to this world, but be transformed by the renewing of your mind, so that you may prove what the will of God is, that which is good and acceptable and perfect.

                        Romans 12:2

Knowing God's Will
NASB

Jeremiah 29:11-13

"I know the plans that I have for you," declares the LORD, "plans for welfare and not for calamity to give you a future and a hope. Then you will call upon Me and come and pray to Me, and I will listen to you. You will seek Me and find Me when you search for Me with all your heart."

                        Jeremiah 29:11-13

Knowing God's Will
NASB

1 John 5:14-15

This is the confidence which we have before Him, that, if we ask anything according to His will, He hears us. And if we know that He hears us in whatever we ask, we know that we have the requests which we have asked from Him.

                        1 John 5:14-15

Knowing God's Will
NASB

Isaiah 30:21

Your ears will hear a word behind you, "This is the way, walk in it," whenever you turn to the right or to the left.

                        Isaiah 30:21

Self-Image
NASB

1 Samuel 16:7

God sees not as man sees, for man looks at the outward appearance, but the LORD looks at the heart.

                        1 Samuel 16:7

Self-Image
NASB

Psalm 139:13-14

For You formed my inward parts;
    You wove me in my mother's womb.
I will give thanks to You, for I am fearfully and
    wonderfully made.

                        Psalm 139:13-14

Self-Image
NASB

Philippians 2:3-5

Do nothing from selfishness or empty conceit, but with humility of mind regard one another as more important than yourselves; do not merely look out for your own personal interests, but also for the interests of others. Have this attitude in yourselves which was also in Christ Jesus.

                        Philippians 2:3-5

Self-Image
NASB

Jeremiah 9:23-24

Thus says the LORD, "Let not a wise man boast of his wisdom, and let not the mighty man boast of his might, let not a rich man boast of his riches; but let him who boasts boast of this, that he understands and knows Me."

                        Jeremiah 9:23-24

Knowing God's Will
KJV

Proverbs 16:9

A man's heart deviseth his way: but the LORD directeth his steps.

Proverbs 16:9

Knowing God's Will
KJV

Proverbs 3:5-7

Trust in the LORD with all thine heart; and lean not unto thine own understanding. In all thy ways acknowledge him, and he shall direct thy paths. Be not wise in thine own eyes: fear the LORD, and depart from evil.

Proverbs 3:5-7

Knowing God's Will
KJV

Jeremiah 29:11-13

I know the thoughts that I think toward you, saith the LORD, thoughts of peace, and not of evil, to give you an expected end. Then shall ye call upon me, and ye shall go and pray unto me, and I will hearken unto you. And ye shall seek me, and find me, when ye shall search for me with all your heart.

Jeremiah 29:11-13

Knowing God's Will
KJV

Romans 12:2

Be not conformed to this world: but be ye transformed by the renewing of your mind, that ye may prove what is that good, and acceptable, and perfect, will of God.

Romans 12:2

Knowing God's Will
KJV

Isaiah 30:21

Thine ears shall hear a word behind thee, saying, This is the way, walk ye in it, when ye turn to the right hand, and when ye turn to the left.

Isaiah 30:21

Knowing God's Will
KJV

1 John 5:14-15

This is the confidence that we have in him, that, if we ask any thing according to his will, he heareth us: And if we know that he hear us, whatsoever we ask, we know that we have the petitions that we desired of him.

1 John 5:14-15

Self-Image
KJV

Psalm 139:13-14

Thou hast possessed my reins: thou hast covered me in my mother's womb. I will praise thee; for I am fearfully and wonderfully made.

Psalm 139:13-14

Self-Image
KJV

1 Samuel 16:7

The LORD seeth not as man seeth; for man looketh on the outward appearance, but the LORD looketh on the heart.

1 Samuel 16:7

Self-Image
KJV

Jeremiah 9:23-24

Thus saith the LORD, Let not the wise man glory in his wisdom, neither let the mighty man glory in his might, let not the rich man glory in his riches: But let him that glorieth glory in this, that he understandeth and knoweth me.

Jeremiah 9:23-24

Self-Image
KJV

Philippians 2:3-5

Let nothing be done through strife or vainglory; but in lowliness of mind let each esteem other better than themselves. Look not every man on his own things, but every man also on the things of others. Let this mind be in you, which was also in Christ Jesus.

Philippians 2:3-5

Knowing God's Will
NIV

Proverbs 3:5-7

Trust in the LORD with all your heart
    and lean not on your own understanding;
in all your ways acknowledge him,
    and he will make your paths straight.
Do not be wise in your own eyes;
    fear the LORD and shun evil.

Proverbs 3:5-7

Knowing God's Will
NIV

Proverbs 16:9

In his heart a man plans his course,
    but the LORD determines his steps.

Proverbs 16:9

Knowing God's Will
NIV

Romans 12:2

Do not conform any longer to the pattern of this world, but be transformed by the renewing of your mind. Then you will be able to test and approve what God's will is—his good, pleasing and perfect will.

Romans 12:2

Knowing God's Will
NIV

Jeremiah 29:11-13

"I know the plans I have for you," declares the LORD, "plans to prosper you and not to harm you, plans to give you hope and a future. Then you will call upon me and come and pray to me, and I will listen to you. You will seek me and find me when you seek me with all your heart."

Jeremiah 29:11-13

Knowing God's Will
NIV

1 John 5:14-15

This is the confidence we have in approaching God: that if we ask anything according to his will, he hears us. And if we know that he hears us—whatever we ask—we know that we have what we asked of him.

1 John 5:14-15

Knowing God's Will
NIV

Isaiah 30:21

Whether you turn to the right or to the left, your ears will hear a voice behind you, saying, "This is the way; walk in it."

Isaiah 30:21

Self-Image
NIV

1 Samuel 16:7

The LORD does not look at the things man looks at. Man looks at the outward appearance, but the LORD looks at the heart.

1 Samuel 16:7

Self-Image
NIV

Psalm 139:13-14

You created my inmost being;
    you knit me together in my mother's womb.
I praise you because I am fearfully and
    wonderfully made.

Psalm 139:13-14

Self-Image
NIV

Philippians 2:3-5

Do nothing out of selfish ambition or vain conceit, but in humility consider others better than yourselves. Each of you should look not only to your own interests, but also to the interests of others. Your attitude should be the same as that of Christ Jesus.

Philippians 2:3-5

Self-Image
NIV

Jeremiah 9:23-24

This is what the LORD says:
    "Let not the wise man boast of his wisdom
    or the strong man boast of his strength
    or the rich man boast of his riches,
but let him who boasts boast about this:
    that he understands and knows me."

Jeremiah 9:23-24

Knowing God's Will
NLT

Proverbs 16:9

We can make our plans,
    but the LORD determines our steps.

Proverbs 16:9

Knowing God's Will
NLT

Proverbs 3:5-7

Trust in the LORD with all your heart;
    do not depend on your own understanding.
Seek his will in all you do,
    and he will show you which path to take.
Don't be impressed with your own wisdom.
    Instead, fear the LORD and turn away from
        evil.

Proverbs 3:5-7

Knowing God's Will
NLT

Jeremiah 29:11-13

"I know the plans I have for you," says the LORD.
"They are plans for good and not for disaster,
to give you a future and a hope. In those days
when you pray, I will listen. If you look for me
wholeheartedly, you will find me."

Jeremiah 29:11-13

Knowing God's Will
NLT

Romans 12:2

Don't copy the behavior and customs of this
world, but let God transform you into a new
person by changing the way you think. Then you
will learn to know God's will for you, which is good
and pleasing and perfect.

Romans 12:2

Knowing God's Will
NLT

Isaiah 30:21

Your own ears will hear him.
    Right behind you a voice will say,
"This is the way you should go,"
    whether to the right or to the left.

Isaiah 30:21

Knowing God's Will
NLT

1 John 5:14-15

And we are confident that he hears us whenever
we ask for anything that pleases him. And since
we know he hears us when we make our requests,
we also know that he will give us what we ask
for.

1 John 5:14-15

Self-Image
NLT

Psalm 139:13-14

You made all the delicate, inner parts of my body
    and knit me together in my mother's womb.
Thank you for making me so wonderfully
    complex!

Psalm 139:13-14

Self-Image
NLT

1 Samuel 16:7

The LORD doesn't see things the way you see
them. People judge by outward appearance, but
the LORD looks at the heart.

1 Samuel 16:7

Self-Image
NLT

Jeremiah 9:23-24

This is what the LORD says:
"Don't let the wise boast in their wisdom,
    or the powerful boast in their power,
    or the rich boast in their riches.
But those who wish to boast
    should boast in this alone:
that they truly know me and understand that I am the
    LORD."

Jeremiah 9:23-24

Self-Image
NLT

Philippians 2:3-5

Don't be selfish; don't try to impress others.
Be humble, thinking of others as better than
yourselves. Don't look out only for your own
interests, but take an interest in others, too. You
must have the same attitude that Christ Jesus
had.

Philippians 2:3-5

Knowing God's Will
ESV

Proverbs 3:5-7

Trust in the LORD with all your heart,
    and do not lean on your own understanding.
In all your ways acknowledge him,
    and he will make straight your paths.
Be not wise in your own eyes;
    fear the LORD, and turn away from evil.

Proverbs 3:5-7

Knowing God's Will
ESV

Proverbs 16:9

The heart of man plans his way,
    but the LORD establishes his steps.

Proverbs 16:9

Knowing God's Will
ESV

Romans 12:2

Do not be conformed to this world, but be transformed by the renewal of your mind, that by testing you may discern what is the will of God, what is good and acceptable and perfect.

Romans 12:2

Knowing God's Will
ESV

Jeremiah 29:11-13

I know the plans I have for you, declares the LORD, plans for welfare and not for evil, to give you a future and a hope. Then you will call upon me and come and pray to me, and I will hear you. You will seek me and find me, when you seek me with all your heart.

Jeremiah 29:11-13

Knowing God's Will
ESV

1 John 5:14-15

And this is the confidence that we have toward him, that if we ask anything according to his will he hears us. And if we know that he hears us in whatever we ask, we know that we have the requests that we have asked of him.

1 John 5:14-15

Knowing God's Will
ESV

Isaiah 30:21

And your ears shall hear a word behind you, saying, "This is the way, walk in it," when you turn to the right or when you turn to the left.

Isaiah 30:21

Self-Image
ESV

1 Samuel 16:7

The LORD sees not as man sees: man looks on the outward appearance, but the LORD looks on the heart.

1 Samuel 16:7

Self-Image
ESV

Psalm 139:13-14

For you formed my inward parts;
    you knitted me together in my mother's
        womb.
I praise you, for I am fearfully and wonderfully
        made.

Psalm 139:13-14

Self-Image
ESV

Philippians 2:3-5

Do nothing from rivalry or conceit, but in humility count others more significant than yourselves. Let each of you look not only to his own interests, but also to the interests of others. Have this mind among yourselves, which is yours in Christ Jesus.

Philippians 2:3-5

Self-Image
ESV

Jeremiah 9:23-24

Thus says the LORD: "Let not the wise man boast in his wisdom, let not the mighty man boast in his might, let not the rich man boast in his riches, but let him who boasts boast in this, that he understands and knows me."

Jeremiah 9:23-24

Self-Image
NKJV

1 Peter 3:3-4

Do not let your adornment be merely outward—arranging the hair, wearing gold, or putting on fine apparel—rather let it be the hidden person of the heart, with the incorruptible beauty of a gentle and quiet spirit, which is very precious in the sight of God.

1 Peter 3:3-4

Self-Image
NKJV

Matthew 10:29-31

Are not two sparrows sold for a copper coin? And not one of them falls to the ground apart from your Father's will. But the very hairs of your head are all numbered. Do not fear therefore; you are of more value than many sparrows.

Matthew 10:29-31

Dealing with Sin
NKJV

1 John 1:8-9

If we say that we have no sin, we deceive ourselves, and the truth is not in us. If we confess our sins, He is faithful and just to forgive us our sins and to cleanse us from all unrighteousness.

1 John 1:8-9

Dealing with Sin
NKJV

1 Corinthians 10:13

No temptation has overtaken you except such as is common to man; but God is faithful, who will not allow you to be tempted beyond what you are able, but with the temptation will also make the way of escape, that you may be able to bear it.

1 Corinthians 10:13

Dealing with Sin
NKJV

Romans 6:11-13

Reckon yourselves to be dead indeed to sin, but alive to God in Christ Jesus our Lord. Therefore do not let sin reign in your mortal body, that you should obey it in its lusts. And do not present your members as instruments of unrighteousness to sin, but present yourselves to God as being alive from the dead, and your members as instruments of righteousness to God.

Romans 6:11-13

Dealing with Sin
NKJV

Galatians 6:1-2

If a man is overtaken in any trespass, you who are spiritual restore such a one in a spirit of gentleness, considering yourself lest you also be tempted. Bear one another's burdens, and so fulfill the law of Christ.

Galatians 6:1-2

Dealing with Sin
NKJV

James 4:7-8

Therefore submit to God. Resist the devil and he will flee from you. Draw near to God and He will draw near to you. Cleanse your hands, you sinners; and purify your hearts, you double-minded.

James 4:7-8

Dealing with Sin
NKJV

Ephesians 6:10-12

Be strong in the Lord and in the power of His might. Put on the whole armor of God, that you may be able to stand against the wiles of the devil. For we do not wrestle against flesh and blood, but against principalities, against powers, against the rulers of the darkness of this age, against spiritual hosts of wickedness in the heavenly places.

Ephesians 6:10-12

Guilt
NKJV

Romans 8:1-2

There is therefore now no condemnation to those who are in Christ Jesus, who do not walk according to the flesh, but according to the Spirit. For the law of the Spirit of life in Christ Jesus has made me free from the law of sin and death.

Romans 8:1-2

Guilt
NKJV

Psalm 51:9-10

Hide Your face from my sins,
    And blot out all my iniquities.
Create in me a clean heart, O God,
    And renew a steadfast spirit within me.

Psalm 51:9-10

Self-Image
NASB

Matthew 10:29-31

Are not two sparrows sold for a cent? And yet not one of them will fall to the ground apart from your Father. But the very hairs of your head are all numbered. So do not fear; you are more valuable than many sparrows.

Matthew 10:29-31

Self-Image
NASB

1 Peter 3:3-4

Your adornment must not be merely external—braiding the hair, and wearing gold jewelry, or putting on dresses; but let it be the hidden person of the heart, with the imperishable quality of a gentle and quiet spirit, which is precious in the sight of God.

1 Peter 3:3-4

Dealing with Sin
NASB

1 Corinthians 10:13

No temptation has overtaken you but such as is common to man; and God is faithful, who will not allow you to be tempted beyond what you are able, but with the temptation will provide the way of escape also, so that you will be able to endure it.

1 Corinthians 10:13

Dealing with Sin
NASB

1 John 1:8-9

If we say that we have no sin, we are deceiving ourselves and the truth is not in us. If we confess our sins, He is faithful and righteous to forgive us our sins and to cleanse us from all unrighteousness.

1 John 1:8-9

Dealing with Sin
NASB

Galatians 6:1-2

Even if anyone is caught in any trespass, you who are spiritual, restore such a one in a spirit of gentleness; each one looking to yourself, so that you too will not be tempted. Bear one another's burdens, and thereby fulfill the law of Christ.

Galatians 6:1-2

Dealing with Sin
NASB

Romans 6:11-13

Consider yourselves to be dead to sin, but alive to God in Christ Jesus. Therefore do not let sin reign in your mortal body so that you obey its lusts, and do not go on presenting the members of your body to sin as instruments of unrighteousness; but present yourselves to God as those alive from the dead, and your members as instruments of righteousness to God.

Romans 6:11-13

Dealing with Sin
NASB

Ephesians 6:10-12

Be strong in the Lord and in the strength of His might. Put on the full armor of God, so that you will be able to stand firm against the schemes of the devil. For our struggle is not against flesh and blood, but against the rulers, against the powers, against the world forces of this darkness, against the spiritual forces of wickedness in the heavenly places.

Ephesians 6:10-12

Dealing with Sin
NASB

James 4:7-8

Submit therefore to God. Resist the devil and he will flee from you. Draw near to God and He will draw near to you. Cleanse your hands, you sinners; and purify your hearts, you double-minded.

James 4:7-8

Guilt
NASB

Psalm 51:9-10

Hide Your face from my sins
    And blot out all my iniquities.
Create in me a clean heart, O God,
    And renew a steadfast spirit within me.

Psalm 51:9-10

Guilt
NASB

Romans 8:1-2

Therefore there is now no condemnation for those who are in Christ Jesus. For the law of the Spirit of life in Christ Jesus has set you free from the law of sin and of death.

Romans 8:1-2

Self-Image
KJV

1 Peter 3:3-4

Whose adorning let it not be that outward adorning of plaiting the hair, and of wearing of gold, or of putting on of apparel; But let it be the hidden man of the heart, in that which is not corruptible, even the ornament of a meek and quiet spirit, which is in the sight of God of great price.

1 Peter 3:3-4

Self-Image
KJV

Matthew 10:29-31

Are not two sparrows sold for a farthing? and one of them shall not fall on the ground without your Father. But the very hairs of your head are all numbered. Fear ye not therefore, ye are of more value than many sparrows.

Matthew 10:29-31

Dealing with Sin
KJV

1 John 1:8-9

If we say that we have no sin, we deceive ourselves, and the truth is not in us. If we confess our sins, he is faithful and just to forgive us our sins, and to cleanse us from all unrighteousness.

1 John 1:8-9

Dealing with Sin
KJV

1 Corinthians 10:13

There hath no temptation taken you but such as is common to man: but God is faithful, who will not suffer you to be tempted above that ye are able; but will with the temptation also make a way to escape, that ye may be able to bear it.

1 Corinthians 10:13

Dealing with Sin
KJV

Romans 6:11-13

Reckon ye also yourselves to be dead indeed unto sin, but alive unto God through Jesus Christ our Lord. Let not sin therefore reign in your mortal body, that ye should obey it in the lusts thereof. Neither yield ye your members as instruments of unrighteousness unto sin: but yield yourselves unto God, as those that are alive from the dead, and your members as instruments of righteousness unto God.

Romans 6:11-13

Dealing with Sin
KJV

Galatians 6:1-2

If a man be overtaken in a fault, ye which are spiritual, restore such an one in the spirit of meekness; considering thyself, lest thou also be tempted. Bear ye one another's burdens, and so fulfil the law of Christ.

Galatians 6:1-2

Dealing with Sin
KJV

James 4:7-8

Submit yourselves therefore to God. Resist the devil, and he will flee from you. Draw nigh to God, and he will draw nigh to you. Cleanse your hands, ye sinners; and purify your hearts, ye double minded.

James 4:7-8

Dealing with Sin
KJV

Ephesians 6:10-12

Be strong in the Lord, and in the power of his might. Put on the whole armour of God, that ye may be able to stand against the wiles of the devil. For we wrestle not against flesh and blood, but against principalities, against powers, against the rulers of the darkness of this world, against spiritual wickedness in high places.

Ephesians 6:10-12

Guilt
KJV

Romans 8:1-2

There is therefore now no condemnation to them which are in Christ Jesus, who walk not after the flesh, but after the Spirit. For the law of the Spirit of life in Christ Jesus hath made me free from the law of sin and death.

Romans 8:1-2

Guilt
KJV

Psalm 51:9-10

Hide thy face from my sins, and blot out all mine iniquities. Create in me a clean heart, O God; and renew a right spirit within me.

Psalm 51:9-10

Self-Image NIV

Matthew 10:29-31

Are not two sparrows sold for a penny? Yet not one of them will fall to the ground apart from the will of your Father. And even the very hairs of your head are all numbered. So don't be afraid; you are worth more than many sparrows.

Matthew 10:29-31

Self-Image NIV

1 Peter 3:3-4

Your beauty should not come from outward adornment, such as braided hair and the wearing of gold jewelry and fine clothes. Instead, it should be that of your inner self, the unfading beauty of a gentle and quiet spirit, which is of great worth in God's sight.

1 Peter 3:3-4

Dealing with Sin NIV

1 Corinthians 10:13

No temptation has seized you except what is common to man. And God is faithful; he will not let you be tempted beyond what you can bear. But when you are tempted, he will also provide a way out so that you can stand up under it.

1 Corinthians 10:13

Dealing with Sin NIV

1 John 1:8-9

If we claim to be without sin, we deceive ourselves and the truth is not in us. If we confess our sins, he is faithful and just and will forgive us our sins and purify us from all unrighteousness.

1 John 1:8-9

Dealing with Sin NIV

Galatians 6:1-2

If someone is caught in a sin, you who are spiritual should restore him gently. But watch yourself, or you also may be tempted. Carry each other's burdens, and in this way you will fulfill the law of Christ.

Galatians 6:1-2

Dealing with Sin NIV

Romans 6:11-13

Count yourselves dead to sin but alive to God in Christ Jesus. Therefore do not let sin reign in your mortal body so that you obey its evil desires. Do not offer the parts of your body to sin, as instruments of wickedness, but rather offer yourselves to God, as those who have been brought from death to life; and offer the parts of your body to him as instruments of righteousness.

Romans 6:11-13

Dealing with Sin NIV

Ephesians 6:10-12

Be strong in the Lord and in his mighty power. Put on the full armor of God so that you can take your stand against the devil's schemes. For our struggle is not against flesh and blood, but against the rulers, against the authorities, against the powers of this dark world and against the spiritual forces of evil in the heavenly realms.

Ephesians 6:10-12

Dealing with Sin NIV

James 4:7-8

Submit yourselves, then, to God. Resist the devil, and he will flee from you. Come near to God and he will come near to you. Wash your hands, you sinners, and purify your hearts, you double-minded.

James 4:7-8

Guilt NIV

Psalm 51:9-10

Hide your face from my sins
  and blot out all my iniquity.
Create in me a pure heart, O God,
  and renew a steadfast spirit within me.

Psalm 51:9-10

Guilt NIV

Romans 8:1-2

There is now no condemnation for those who are in Christ Jesus, because through Christ Jesus the law of the Spirit of life set me free from the law of sin and death.

Romans 8:1-2

Self-Image

NLT

1 Peter 3:3-4

Don't be concerned about the outward beauty of fancy hairstyles, expensive jewelry, or beautiful clothes. You should clothe yourselves instead with the beauty that comes from within, the unfading beauty of a gentle and quiet spirit, which is so precious to God.

1 Peter 3:3-4

Self-Image

NLT

Matthew 10:29-31

What is the price of two sparrows—one copper coin? But not a single sparrow can fall to the ground without your Father knowing it. And the very hairs on your head are all numbered. So don't be afraid; you are more valuable to God than a whole flock of sparrows.

Matthew 10:29-31

Dealing with Sin

NLT

1 John 1:8-9

If we claim we have no sin, we are only fooling ourselves and not living in the truth. But if we confess our sins to him, he is faithful and just to forgive us our sins and to cleanse us from all wickedness.

1 John 1:8-9

Dealing with Sin

NLT

1 Corinthians 10:13

The temptations in your life are no different from what others experience. And God is faithful. He will not allow the temptation to be more than you can stand. When you are tempted, he will show you a way out so that you can endure.

1 Corinthians 10:13

Dealing with Sin

NLT

Romans 6:11-13

You also should consider yourselves to be dead to the power of sin and alive to God through Christ Jesus. Do not let sin control the way you live; do not give in to sinful desires. Do not let any part of your body become an instrument of evil to serve sin. Instead, give yourselves completely to God, for you were dead, but now you have new life. So use your whole body as an instrument to do what is right for the glory of God.

Romans 6:11-13

Dealing with Sin

NLT

Galatians 6:1-2

If another believer is overcome by some sin, you who are godly should gently and humbly help that person back onto the right path. And be careful not to fall into the same temptation yourself. Share each other's burdens, and in this way obey the law of Christ.

Galatians 6:1-2

Dealing with Sin

NLT

James 4:7-8

So humble yourselves before God. Resist the devil, and he will flee from you. Come close to God, and God will come close to you. Wash your hands, you sinners; purify your hearts, for your loyalty is divided between God and the world.

James 4:7-8

Dealing with Sin

NLT

Ephesians 6:10-12

Be strong in the Lord and in his mighty power. Put on all of God's armor so that you will be able to stand firm against all strategies of the devil. For we are not fighting against flesh-and-blood enemies, but against evil rulers and authorities of the unseen world, against mighty powers in this dark world, and against evil spirits in the heavenly places.

Ephesians 6:10-12

Guilt

NLT

Romans 8:1-2

So now there is no condemnation for those who belong to Christ Jesus. And because you belong to him, the power of the life-giving Spirit has freed you from the power of sin that leads to death.

Romans 8:1-2

Guilt

NLT

Psalm 51:9-10

Don't keep looking at my sins.
    Remove the stain of my guilt.
Create in me a clean heart, O God.
    Renew a loyal spirit within me.

Psalm 51:9-10

Self-Image ESV

Matthew 10:29-31

Are not two sparrows sold for a penny? And not one of them will fall to the ground apart from your Father. But even the hairs of your head are all numbered. Fear not, therefore; you are of more value than many sparrows.

Matthew 10:29-31

Self-Image ESV

1 Peter 3:3-4

Do not let your adorning be external—the braiding of hair and the putting on of gold jewelry, or the clothing you wear—but let your adorning be the hidden person of the heart with the imperishable beauty of a gentle and quiet spirit, which in God's sight is very precious.

1 Peter 3:3-4

Dealing with Sin ESV

1 Corinthians 10:13

No temptation has overtaken you that is not common to man. God is faithful, and he will not let you be tempted beyond your ability, but with the temptation he will also provide the way of escape, that you may be able to endure it.

1 Corinthians 10:13

Dealing with Sin ESV

1 John 1:8-9

If we say we have no sin, we deceive ourselves, and the truth is not in us. If we confess our sins, he is faithful and just to forgive us our sins and to cleanse us from all unrighteousness.

1 John 1:8-9

Dealing with Sin ESV

Galatians 6:1-2

If anyone is caught in any transgression, you who are spiritual should restore him in a spirit of gentleness. Keep watch on yourself, lest you too be tempted. Bear one another's burdens, and so fulfill the law of Christ.

Galatians 6:1-2

Dealing with Sin ESV

Romans 6:11-13

You also must consider yourselves dead to sin and alive to God in Christ Jesus. Let not sin therefore reign in your mortal body, to make you obey its passions. Do not present your members to sin as instruments for unrighteousness, but present yourselves to God as those who have been brought from death to life, and your members to God as instruments for righteousness.

Romans 6:11-13

Dealing with Sin ESV

Ephesians 6:10-12

Be strong in the Lord and in the strength of his might. Put on the whole armor of God, that you may be able to stand against the schemes of the devil. For we do not wrestle against flesh and blood, but against the rulers, against the authorities, against the cosmic powers over this present darkness, against the spiritual forces of evil in the heavenly places.

Ephesians 6:10-12

Dealing with Sin ESV

James 4:7-8

Submit yourselves therefore to God. Resist the devil, and he will flee from you. Draw near to God, and he will draw near to you. Cleanse your hands, you sinners, and purify your hearts, you double-minded.

James 4:7-8

Guilt ESV

Psalm 51:9-10

Hide your face from my sins,
    and blot out all my iniquities.
Create in me a clean heart, O God,
    and renew a right spirit within me.

Psalm 51:9-10

Guilt ESV

Romans 8:1-2

There is therefore now no condemnation for those who are in Christ Jesus. For the law of the Spirit of life has set you free in Christ Jesus from the law of sin and death.

Romans 8:1-2

Guilt
NKJV

Proverbs 28:13

He who covers his sins will not prosper,
But whoever confesses and forsakes them
will have mercy.

Proverbs 28:13

Guilt
NKJV

Psalm 32:1-2

Blessed is he whose transgression is forgiven,
Whose sin is covered.
Blessed is the man to whom the LORD does not
impute iniquity,
And in whose spirit there is no deceit.

Psalm 32:1-2

Guilt
NKJV

2 Corinthians 7:10

Godly sorrow produces repentance leading to
salvation, not to be regretted; but the sorrow of
the world produces death.

2 Corinthians 7:10

Guilt
NKJV

James 5:16

Confess your trespasses to one another, and pray
for one another, that you may be healed. The
effective, fervent prayer of a righteous man avails
much.

James 5:16

Perfectionism
NKJV

Galatians 3:3

Are you so foolish? Having begun in the Spirit, are
you now being made perfect by the flesh?

Galatians 3:3

Perfectionism
NKJV

Psalm 127:1-2

Unless the LORD builds the house,
They labor in vain who build it;
Unless the LORD guards the city,
The watchman stays awake in vain.
It is vain for you to rise up early,
To sit up late,
To eat the bread of sorrows;
For so He gives His beloved sleep.

Psalm 127:1-2

Perfectionism
NKJV

Ephesians 2:8-9

By grace you have been saved through faith, and
that not of yourselves; it is the gift of God, not of
works, lest anyone should boast.

Ephesians 2:8-9

Perfectionism
NKJV

Ecclesiastes 2:10-11

Whatever my eyes desired I did not keep from them.
I did not withhold my heart from any pleasure,
For my heart rejoiced in all my labor;
And this was my reward from all my labor.
Then I looked on all the works that my hands had done
And on the labor in which I had toiled;
And indeed all was vanity and grasping for the wind.
There was no profit under the sun.

Ecclesiastes 2:10-11

Perfectionism
NKJV

2 Corinthians 12:9

He said to me, "My grace is sufficient for you,
for My strength is made perfect in weakness."
Therefore most gladly I will rather boast in my
infirmities, that the power of Christ may rest upon
me.

2 Corinthians 12:9

Perfectionism
NKJV

Luke 10:40-42

Martha was distracted with much serving, and she
approached Him and said, "Lord, do You not care that
my sister has left me to serve alone? Therefore tell
her to help me." And Jesus answered and said to her,
"Martha, Martha, you are worried and troubled about
many things. But one thing is needed, and Mary has
chosen that good part, which will not be taken away
from her."

Luke 10:40-42

Guilt

Psalm 32:1-2

How blessed is he whose transgression is
    forgiven,
    Whose sin is covered!
How blessed is the man to whom the LORD
    does not impute iniquity,
    And in whose spirit there is no deceit!

Psalm 32:1-2

Guilt

Proverbs 28:13

He who conceals his transgressions will not
    prosper,
    But he who confesses and forsakes them
    will find compassion.

Proverbs 28:13

Guilt

James 5:16

Confess your sins to one another, and pray for one another so that you may be healed. The effective prayer of a righteous man can accomplish much.

James 5:16

Guilt

2 Corinthians 7:10

The sorrow that is according to the will of God produces a repentance without regret, leading to salvation, but the sorrow of the world produces death.

2 Corinthians 7:10

Perfectionism

Psalm 127:1-2

Unless the LORD builds the house,
    They labor in vain who build it;
    Unless the LORD guards the city,
    The watchman keeps awake in vain.
It is vain for you to rise up early,
    To retire late,
    To eat the bread of painful labors;
    For He gives to His beloved even in his sleep.

Psalm 127:1-2

Perfectionism

Galatians 3:3

Are you so foolish? Having begun by the Spirit, are you now being perfected by the flesh?

Galatians 3:3

Perfectionism

Ecclesiastes 2:10-11

All that my eyes desired I did not refuse them. I did not withhold my heart from any pleasure, for my heart was pleased because of all my labor and this was my reward for all my labor. Thus I considered all my activities which my hands had done and the labor which I had exerted, and behold all was vanity and striving after wind and there was no profit under the sun.

Ecclesiastes 2:10-11

Perfectionism

Ephesians 2:8-9

By grace you have been saved through faith; and that not of yourselves, it is the gift of God; not as a result of works, so that no one may boast.

Ephesians 2:8-9

Perfectionism

Luke 10:40-42

Martha was distracted with all her preparations; and she came up to Him and said, "Lord, do You not care that my sister has left me to do all the serving alone? Then tell her to help me." But the Lord answered and said to her, "Martha, Martha, you are worried and bothered about so many things; but only one thing is necessary, for Mary has chosen the good part, which shall not be taken away from her."

Luke 10:40-42

Perfectionism

2 Corinthians 12:9

He has said to me, "My grace is sufficient for you, for power is perfected in weakness." Most gladly, therefore, I will rather boast about my weaknesses, so that the power of Christ may dwell in me.

2 Corinthians 12:9

Guilt
KJV

Proverbs 28:13

He that covereth his sins shall not prosper: but whoso confesseth and forsaketh them shall have mercy.

Proverbs 28:13

Guilt
KJV

Psalm 32:1-2

Blessed is he whose transgression is forgiven, whose sin is covered. Blessed is the man unto whom the Lord imputeth not iniquity, and in whose spirit there is no guile.

Psalm 32:1-2

Guilt
KJV

2 Corinthians 7:10

Godly sorrow worketh repentance to salvation not to be repented of: but the sorrow of the world worketh death.

2 Corinthians 7:10

Guilt
KJV

James 5:16

Confess your faults one to another, and pray one for another, that ye may be healed. The effectual fervent prayer of a righteous man availeth much.

James 5:16

Perfectionism
KJV

Galatians 3:3

Are ye so foolish? having begun in the Spirit, are ye now made perfect by the flesh?

Galatians 3:3

Perfectionism
KJV

Psalm 127:1-2

Except the Lord build the house, they labour in vain that build it: except the Lord keep the city, the watchman waketh but in vain. It is vain for you to rise up early, to sit up late, to eat the bread of sorrows: for so he giveth his beloved sleep.

Psalm 127:1-2

Perfectionism
KJV

Ephesians 2:8-9

By grace are ye saved through faith; and that not of yourselves: it is the gift of God: Not of works, lest any man should boast.

Ephesians 2:8-9

Perfectionism
KJV

Ecclesiastes 2:10-11

Whatsoever mine eyes desired I kept not from them, I withheld not my heart from any joy; for my heart rejoiced in all my labour: and this was my portion of all my labour. Then I looked on all the works that my hands had wrought, and on the labour that I had laboured to do: and, behold, all was vanity and vexation of spirit, and there was no profit under the sun.

Ecclesiastes 2:10-11

Perfectionism
KJV

2 Corinthians 12:9

He said unto me, My grace is sufficient for thee: for my strength is made perfect in weakness. Most gladly therefore will I rather glory in my infirmities, that the power of Christ may rest upon me.

2 Corinthians 12:9

Perfectionism
KJV

Luke 10:40-42

Martha was cumbered about much serving, and came to him, and said, Lord, dost thou not care that my sister hath left me to serve alone? bid her therefore that she help me. And Jesus answered and said unto her, Martha, Martha, thou art careful and troubled about many things: But one thing is needful: and Mary hath chosen that good part, which shall not be taken away from her.

Luke 10:40-42

Guilt
NIV

Psalm 32:1-2

Blessed is he
    whose transgressions are forgiven,
    whose sins are covered.
Blessed is the man
    whose sin the LORD does not count against
      him
    and in whose spirit is no deceit.

Psalm 32:1-2

Guilt
NIV

Proverbs 28:13

He who conceals his sins does not prosper,
    but whoever confesses and renounces
      them finds mercy.

Proverbs 28:13

Guilt
NIV

James 5:16

Confess your sins to each other and pray for each other so that you may be healed. The prayer of a righteous man is powerful and effective.

James 5:16

Guilt
NIV

2 Corinthians 7:10

Godly sorrow brings repentance that leads to salvation and leaves no regret, but worldly sorrow brings death.

2 Corinthians 7:10

Perfectionism
NIV

Psalm 127:1-2

Unless the LORD builds the house,
    its builders labor in vain.
    Unless the LORD watches over the city,
    the watchmen stand guard in vain.
In vain you rise early
    and stay up late,
    toiling for food to eat —
    for he grants sleep to those he loves.

Psalm 127:1-2

Perfectionism
NIV

Galatians 3:3

Are you so foolish? After beginning with the Spirit, are you now trying to attain your goal by human effort?

Galatians 3:3

Perfectionism
NIV

Ecclesiastes 2:10-11

I denied myself nothing my eyes desired;
    I refused my heart no pleasure.
    My heart took delight in all my work,
    and this was the reward for all my labor.
Yet when I surveyed all that my hands had done
    and what I had toiled to achieve,
    everything was meaningless, a chasing after the wind;
    nothing was gained under the sun.

Ecclesiastes 2:10-11

Perfectionism
NIV

Ephesians 2:8-9

It is by grace you have been saved, through faith — and this not from yourselves, it is the gift of God — not by works, so that no one can boast.

Ephesians 2:8-9

Perfectionism
NIV

Luke 10:40-42

Martha was distracted by all the preparations that had to be made. She came to him and asked, "Lord, don't you care that my sister has left me to do the work by myself? Tell her to help me!"

"Martha, Martha," the Lord answered, "you are worried and upset about many things, but only one thing is needed. Mary has chosen what is better, and it will not be taken away from her."

Luke 10:40-42

Perfectionism
NIV

2 Corinthians 12:9

He said to me, "My grace is sufficient for you, for my power is made perfect in weakness." Therefore I will boast all the more gladly about my weaknesses, so that Christ's power may rest on me.

2 Corinthians 12:9

Guilt
NLT

Proverbs 28:13

People who conceal their sins will not prosper,
but if they confess and turn from them,
they will receive mercy.

Proverbs 28:13

Guilt
NLT

Psalm 32:1-2

Oh, what joy for those
whose disobedience is forgiven,
whose sin is put out of sight!
Yes, what joy for those
whose record the LORD has cleared of guilt,
whose lives are lived in complete honesty!

Psalm 32:1-2

Guilt
NLT

2 Corinthians 7:10

The kind of sorrow God wants us to experience leads us away from sin and results in salvation. There's no regret for that kind of sorrow. But worldly sorrow, which lacks repentance, results in spiritual death.

2 Corinthians 7:10

Guilt
NLT

James 5:16

Confess your sins to each other and pray for each other so that you may be healed. The earnest prayer of a righteous person has great power and produces wonderful results.

James 5:16

Perfectionism
NLT

Galatians 3:3

How foolish can you be? After starting your Christian lives in the Spirit, why are you now trying to become perfect by your own human effort?

Galatians 3:3

Perfectionism
NLT

Psalm 127:1-2

Unless the LORD builds a house,
the work of the builders is wasted.
Unless the LORD protects a city,
guarding it with sentries will do no good.
It is useless for you to work so hard
from early morning until late at night,
anxiously working for food to eat;
for God gives rest to his loved ones.

Psalm 127:1-2

Perfectionism
NLT

Ephesians 2:8-9

God saved you by his grace when you believed. And you can't take credit for this; it is a gift from God. Salvation is not a reward for the good things we have done, so none of us can boast about it.

Ephesians 2:8-9

Perfectionism
NLT

Ecclesiastes 2:10-11

Anything I wanted, I would take. I denied myself no pleasure. I even found great pleasure in hard work, a reward for all my labors. But as I looked at everything I had worked so hard to accomplish, it was all so meaningless—like chasing the wind. There was nothing really worthwhile anywhere.

Ecclesiastes 2:10-11

Perfectionism
NLT

2 Corinthians 12:9

He said, "My grace is all you need. My power works best in weakness." So now I am glad to boast about my weaknesses, so that the power of Christ can work through me.

2 Corinthians 12:9

Perfectionism
NLT

Luke 10:40-42

But Martha was distracted by the big dinner she was preparing. She came to Jesus and said, "Lord, doesn't it seem unfair to you that my sister just sits here while I do all the work? Tell her to come and help me." But the Lord said to her, "My dear Martha, you are worried and upset over all these details! There is only one thing worth being concerned about. Mary has discovered it, and it will not be taken away from her."

Luke 10:40-42

Guilt
ESV

Psalm 32:1-2

Blessed is the one whose transgression is
    forgiven,
    whose sin is covered.
Blessed is the man against whom the Lord
    counts no iniquity,
    and in whose spirit there is no deceit.

Psalm 32:1-2

Guilt
ESV

Proverbs 28:13

Whoever conceals his transgressions will not
    prosper,
    but he who confesses and forsakes them
    will obtain mercy.

Proverbs 28:13

Guilt
ESV

James 5:16

Confess your sins to one another and pray for
one another, that you may be healed. The prayer
of a righteous person has great power as it is
working.

James 5:16

Guilt
ESV

2 Corinthians 7:10

Godly grief produces a repentance that leads to
salvation without regret, whereas worldly grief
produces death.

2 Corinthians 7:10

Perfectionism
ESV

Psalm 127:1-2

Unless the Lord builds the house,
    those who build it labor in vain.
Unless the Lord watches over the city,
    the watchman stays awake in vain.
It is in vain that you rise up early
    and go late to rest,
eating the bread of anxious toil;
    for he gives to his beloved sleep.

Psalm 127:1-2

Perfectionism
ESV

Galatians 3:3

Are you so foolish? Having begun by the Spirit, are
you now being perfected by the flesh?

Galatians 3:3

Perfectionism
ESV

Ecclesiastes 2:10-11

And whatever my eyes desired I did not keep from them.
I kept my heart from no pleasure, for my heart found
pleasure in all my toil, and this was my reward for all my
toil. Then I considered all that my hands had done and
the toil I had expended in doing it, and behold, all was
vanity and a striving after wind, and there was nothing
to be gained under the sun.

Ecclesiastes 2:10-11

Perfectionism
ESV

Ephesians 2:8-9

By grace you have been saved through faith. And
this is not your own doing; it is the gift of God, not
a result of works, so that no one may boast.

Ephesians 2:8-9

Perfectionism
ESV

Luke 10:40-42

Martha was distracted with much serving. And she went
up to him and said, "Lord, do you not care that my sister
has left me to serve alone? Tell her then to help me."
But the Lord answered her, "Martha, Martha, you are
anxious and troubled about many things, but one thing
is necessary. Mary has chosen the good portion, which
will not be taken away from her."

Luke 10:40-42

Perfectionism
ESV

2 Corinthians 12:9

He said to me, "My grace is sufficient for you, for
my power is made perfect in weakness." Therefore
I will boast all the more gladly of my weaknesses,
so that the power of Christ may rest upon me.

2 Corinthians 12:9

Anger
NKJV

Proverbs 29:11

A fool vents all his feelings,
    But a wise man holds them back.

                      Proverbs 29:11

Anger
NKJV

James 1:19-20

Let every man be swift to hear, slow to speak, slow to wrath; for the wrath of man does not produce the righteousness of God.

                      James 1:19-20

Anger
NKJV

Romans 12:19

Beloved, do not avenge yourselves, but rather give place to wrath; for it is written, "Vengeance is Mine, I will repay," says the Lord.

                      Romans 12:19

Anger
NKJV

Proverbs 15:1

A soft answer turns away wrath,
    But a harsh word stirs up anger.

                      Proverbs 15:1

Anger
NKJV

Colossians 3:8-10

Now you yourselves are to put off all these: anger, wrath, malice, blasphemy, filthy language out of your mouth. Do not lie to one another, since you have put off the old man with his deeds, and have put on the new man who is renewed in knowledge according to the image of Him who created him.

                      Colossians 3:8-10

Anger
NKJV

Ephesians 4:26-27

"Be angry, and do not sin": do not let the sun go down on your wrath, nor give place to the devil.

                      Ephesians 4:26-27

Depression
NKJV

Lamentations 3:19-23

Remember my affliction and roaming,
    The wormwood and the gall.
    My soul still remembers
    And sinks within me.
    This I recall to my mind,
    Therefore I have hope.
    Through the LORD's mercies we are not consumed,
    Because His compassions fail not.
    They are new every morning;
    Great is Your faithfulness.

                      Lamentations 3:19-23

Depression
NKJV

Psalm 42:5

Why are you cast down, O my soul?
    And why are you disquieted within me?
    Hope in God, for I shall yet praise Him
    For the help of His countenance.

                      Psalm 42:5

Depression
NKJV

Isaiah 43:1-2

Fear not, for I have redeemed you;
I have called you by your name;
You are Mine.
When you pass through the waters, I will be with you;
And through the rivers, they shall not overflow you.
When you walk through the fire, you shall not be
    burned,
Nor shall the flame scorch you.

                      Isaiah 43:1-2

Depression
NKJV

2 Corinthians 1:8-9

We were burdened beyond measure, above strength, so that we despaired even of life. Yes, we had the sentence of death in ourselves, that we should not trust in ourselves but in God who raises the dead.

                      2 Corinthians 1:8-9

Anger
NASB

James 1:19-20

Everyone must be quick to hear, slow to speak and slow to anger; for the anger of man does not achieve the righteousness of God.

James 1:19-20

Anger
NASB

Proverbs 29:11

A fool always loses his temper,
But a wise man holds it back.

Proverbs 29:11

Anger
NASB

Proverbs 15:1

A gentle answer turns away wrath,
But a harsh word stirs up anger.

Proverbs 15:1

Anger
NASB

Romans 12:19

Never take your own revenge, beloved, but leave room for the wrath of God, for it is written, "Vengeance is Mine, I will repay," says the Lord.

Romans 12:19

Anger
NASB

Ephesians 4:26-27

Be angry, and yet do not sin; do not let the sun go down on your anger, and do not give the devil an opportunity.

Ephesians 4:26-27

Anger
NASB

Colossians 3:8-10

Now you also, put them all aside: anger, wrath, malice, slander, and abusive speech from your mouth. Do not lie to one another, since you laid aside the old self with its evil practices, and have put on the new self who is being renewed to a true knowledge according to the image of the One who created him.

Colossians 3:8-10

Depression
NASB

Psalm 42:5

Why are you in despair, O my soul?
And why have you become disturbed within me?
Hope in God, for I shall again praise Him
For the help of His presence.

Psalm 42:5

Depression
NASB

Lamentations 3:19-23

Remember my affliction and my wandering, the wormwood and bitterness.
Surely my soul remembers
And is bowed down within me.
This I recall to my mind,
Therefore I have hope.
The Lord's lovingkindnesses indeed never cease,
For His compassions never fail.
They are new every morning;
Great is Your faithfulness.

Lamentations 3:19-23

Depression
NASB

2 Corinthians 1:8-9

We were burdened excessively, beyond our strength, so that we despaired even of life; indeed, we had the sentence of death within ourselves so that we would not trust in ourselves, but in God who raises the dead.

2 Corinthians 1:8-9

Depression
NASB

Isaiah 43:1-2

Do not fear, for I have redeemed you;
I have called you by name; you are Mine!
When you pass through the waters, I will be with you;
And through the rivers, they will not overflow you.
When you walk through the fire, you will not be scorched,
Nor will the flame burn you.

Isaiah 43:1-2

Anger
KJV

Proverbs 29:11

A fool uttereth all his mind: but a wise man keepeth it in till afterwards.

Proverbs 29:11

Anger
KJV

James 1:19-20

Let every man be swift to hear, slow to speak, slow to wrath: For the wrath of man worketh not the righteousness of God.

James 1:19-20

Anger
KJV

Romans 12:19

Dearly beloved, avenge not yourselves, but rather give place unto wrath: for it is written, Vengeance is mine; I will repay, saith the Lord.

Romans 12:19

Anger
KJV

Proverbs 15:1

A soft answer turneth away wrath: but grievous words stir up anger.

Proverbs 15:1

Anger
KJV

Colossians 3:8-10

Now ye also put off all these; anger, wrath, malice, blasphemy, filthy communication out of your mouth. Lie not one to another, seeing that ye have put off the old man with his deeds; And have put on the new man, which is renewed in knowledge after the image of him that created him.

Colossians 3:8-10

Anger
KJV

Ephesians 4:26-27

Be ye angry, and sin not: let not the sun go down upon your wrath: Neither give place to the devil.

Ephesians 4:26-27

Depression
KJV

Lamentations 3:19-23

Remembering mine affliction and my misery, the wormwood and the gall. My soul hath them still in remembrance, and is humbled in me. This I recall to my mind, therefore have I hope. It is of the LORD's mercies that we are not consumed, because his compassions fail not. They are new every morning: great is thy faithfulness.

Lamentations 3:19-23

Depression
KJV

Psalm 42:5

Why art thou cast down, O my soul? and why art thou disquieted in me? hope thou in God: for I shall yet praise him for the help of his countenance.

Psalm 42:5

Depression
KJV

Isaiah 43:1-2

Fear not: for I have redeemed thee, I have called thee by thy name; thou art mine. When thou passest through the waters, I will be with thee; and through the rivers, they shall not overflow thee: when thou walkest through the fire, thou shalt not be burned; neither shall the flame kindle upon thee.

Isaiah 43:1-2

Depression
KJV

2 Corinthians 1:8-9

We were pressed out of measure, above strength, insomuch that we despaired even of life: But we had the sentence of death in ourselves, that we should not trust in ourselves, but in God which raiseth the dead.

2 Corinthians 1:8-9

Anger
NIV

James 1:19-20

Everyone should be quick to listen, slow to speak and slow to become angry, for man's anger does not bring about the righteous life that God desires.

James 1:19-20

Anger
NIV

Proverbs 29:11

A fool gives full vent to his anger,
but a wise man keeps himself under control.

Proverbs 29:11

Anger
NIV

Proverbs 15:1

A gentle answer turns away wrath,
but a harsh word stirs up anger.

Proverbs 15:1

Anger
NIV

Romans 12:19

Do not take revenge, my friends, but leave room for God's wrath, for it is written: "It is mine to avenge; I will repay," says the Lord.

Romans 12:19

Anger
NIV

Ephesians 4:26-27

"In your anger do not sin": Do not let the sun go down while you are still angry, and do not give the devil a foothold.

Ephesians 4:26-27

Anger
NIV

Colossians 3:8-10

Now you must rid yourselves of all such things as these: anger, rage, malice, slander, and filthy language from your lips. Do not lie to each other, since you have taken off your old self with its practices and have put on the new self, which is being renewed in knowledge in the image of its Creator.

Colossians 3:8-10

Depression
NIV

Psalm 42:5-6

Why are you downcast, O my soul?
Why so disturbed within me?
Put your hope in God,
for I will yet praise him,
my Savior and my God.

Psalm 42:5-6

Depression
NIV

Lamentations 3:19-23

I remember my affliction and my wandering,
the bitterness and the gall.
I well remember them,
and my soul is downcast within me.
Yet this I call to mind
and therefore I have hope:
Because of the LORD's great love we are not consumed,
for his compassions never fail.
They are new every morning;
great is your faithfulness.

Lamentations 3:19-23

Depression
NIV

2 Corinthians 1:8-9

We were under great pressure, far beyond our ability to endure, so that we despaired even of life. Indeed, in our hearts we felt the sentence of death. But this happened that we might not rely on ourselves but on God, who raises the dead.

2 Corinthians 1:8-9

Depression
NIV

Isaiah 43:1-2

Fear not, for I have redeemed you;
I have summoned you by name; you are mine.
When you pass through the waters,
I will be with you;
and when you pass through the rivers,
they will not sweep over you.
When you walk through the fire,
you will not be burned;
the flames will not set you ablaze.

Isaiah 43:1-2

Anger
NLT

Proverbs 29:11

Fools vent their anger,
but the wise quietly hold it back.

Proverbs 29:11

Anger
NLT

James 1:19-20

You must all be quick to listen, slow to speak, and slow to get angry. Human anger does not produce the righteousness God desires.

James 1:19-20

Anger
NLT

Romans 12:19

Dear friends, never take revenge. Leave that to the righteous anger of God. For the Scriptures say,

"I will take revenge;
I will pay them back,"
says the Lord.

Romans 12:19

Anger
NLT

Proverbs 15:1

A gentle answer deflects anger,
but harsh words make tempers flare.

Proverbs 15:1

Anger
NLT

Colossians 3:8-10

Now is the time to get rid of anger, rage, malicious behavior, slander, and dirty language. Don't lie to each other, for you have stripped off your old sinful nature and all its wicked deeds. Put on your new nature, and be renewed as you learn to know your Creator and become like him.

Colossians 3:8-10

Anger
NLT

Ephesians 4:26-27

And "don't sin by letting anger control you." Don't let the sun go down while you are still angry, for anger gives a foothold to the devil.

Ephesians 4:26-27

Depression
NLT

Lamentations 3:19-23

The thought of my suffering and homelessness
is bitter beyond words.
I will never forget this awful time,
as I grieve over my loss.
Yet I still dare to hope
when I remember this:
The faithful love of the Lord never ends!
His mercies never cease.
Great is his faithfulness;
his mercies begin afresh each morning.

Lamentations 3:19-23

Depression
NLT

Psalm 42:5-6

Why am I discouraged?
Why is my heart so sad?
I will put my hope in God!
I will praise him again—
my Savior and my God!

Psalm 42:5-6

Depression
NLT

Isaiah 43:1-2

Do not be afraid, for I have ransomed you.
I have called you by name; you are mine.
When you go through deep waters,
I will be with you.
When you go through rivers of difficulty,
you will not drown.
When you walk through the fire of oppression,
you will not be burned up;
the flames will not consume you.

Isaiah 43:1-2

Depression
NLT

2 Corinthians 1:8-9

We were crushed and overwhelmed beyond our ability to endure, and we thought we would never live through it. In fact, we expected to die. But as a result, we stopped relying on ourselves and learned to rely only on God, who raises the dead.

2 Corinthians 1:8-9

Anger
ESV

James 1:19-20

Let every person be quick to hear, slow to speak, slow to anger; for the anger of man does not produce the righteousness of God.

James 1:19-20

Anger
ESV

Proverbs 29:11

A fool gives full vent to his spirit,
   but a wise man quietly holds it back.

Proverbs 29:11

Anger
ESV

Proverbs 15:1

A soft answer turns away wrath,
   but a harsh word stirs up anger.

Proverbs 15:1

Anger
ESV

Romans 12:19

Beloved, never avenge yourselves, but leave it to the wrath of God, for it is written, "Vengeance is mine, I will repay, says the Lord."

Romans 12:19

Anger
ESV

Ephesians 4:26-27

Be angry and do not sin; do not let the sun go down on your anger, and give no opportunity to the devil.

Ephesians 4:26-27

Anger
ESV

Colossians 3:8-10

Now you must put them all away: anger, wrath, malice, slander, and obscene talk from your mouth. Do not lie to one another, seeing that you have put off the old self with its practices and have put on the new self, which is being renewed in knowledge after the image of its creator.

Colossians 3:8-10

Depression
ESV

Psalm 42:5

Why are you cast down, O my soul,
   and why are you in turmoil within me?
Hope in God; for I shall again praise him,
   my salvation.

Psalm 42:5

Depression
ESV

Lamentations 3:19-23

Remember my affliction and my wanderings,
   the wormwood and the gall!
My soul continually remembers it
   and is bowed down within me.
But this I call to mind,
   and therefore I have hope:
The steadfast love of the LORD never ceases;
   his mercies never come to an end;
they are new every morning;
   great is your faithfulness.

Lamentations 3:19-23

Depression
ESV

2 Corinthians 1:8-9

We were so utterly burdened beyond our strength that we despaired of life itself. Indeed, we felt that we had received the sentence of death. But that was to make us rely not on ourselves but on God who raises the dead.

2 Corinthians 1:8-9

Depression
ESV

Isaiah 43:1-2

Fear not, for I have redeemed you;
   I have called you by name, you are mine.
When you pass through the waters, I will be with you;
   and through the rivers, they shall not overwhelm you;
when you walk through fire you shall not be burned,
   and the flame shall not consume you.

Isaiah 43:1-2

Depression NKJV

2 Corinthians 4:8-10

We are hard pressed on every side, yet not crushed; we are perplexed, but not in despair; persecuted, but not forsaken; struck down, but not destroyed—always carrying about in the body the dying of the Lord Jesus, that the life of Jesus also may be manifested in our body.

2 Corinthians 4:8-10

Sex NKJV

Matthew 5:27-28

You have heard that it was said to those of old, "You shall not commit adultery." But I say to you that whoever looks at a woman to lust for her has already committed adultery with her in his heart.

Matthew 5:27-28

Sex NKJV

Ephesians 5:3

Fornication and all uncleanness or covetousness, let it not even be named among you, as is fitting for saints.

Ephesians 5:3

Sex NKJV

Hebrews 13:4

Marriage is honorable among all, and the bed undefiled; but fornicators and adulterers God will judge.

Hebrews 13:4

Money NKJV

Deuteronomy 8:17-18

You say in your heart, "My power and the might of my hand have gained me this wealth." And you shall remember the LORD your God, for it is He who gives you power to get wealth.

Deuteronomy 8:17-18

Depression NKJV

Psalm 34:17-18

The righteous cry out, and the LORD hears,
  And delivers them out of all their troubles.
The LORD is near to those who have a broken
  heart,
    And saves such as have a contrite spirit.

Psalm 34:17-18

Sex NKJV

1 Thessalonians 4:3-5

This is the will of God, your sanctification: that you should abstain from sexual immorality; that each of you should know how to possess his own vessel in sanctification and honor, not in passion of lust, like the Gentiles who do not know God.

1 Thessalonians 4:3-5

Sex NKJV

1 Corinthians 6:18-20

Flee sexual immorality. Every sin that a man does is outside the body, but he who commits sexual immorality sins against his own body. Or do you not know that your body is the temple of the Holy Spirit who is in you, whom you have from God, and you are not your own? For you were bought at a price; therefore glorify God in your body and in your spirit, which are God's.

1 Corinthians 6:18-20

Sex NKJV

Romans 13:13-14

Let us walk properly, as in the day, not in revelry and drunkenness, not in lewdness and lust, not in strife and envy. But put on the Lord Jesus Christ, and make no provision for the flesh, to fulfill its lusts.

Romans 13:13-14

Money NKJV

Matthew 6:19-21

Do not lay up for yourselves treasures on earth, where moth and rust destroy and where thieves break in and steal; but lay up for yourselves treasures in heaven, where neither moth nor rust destroys and where thieves do not break in and steal. For where your treasure is, there your heart will be also.

Matthew 6:19-21

Depression
NASB

Psalm 34:17-18

The righteous cry, and the Lord hears
  And delivers them out of all their troubles.
The Lord is near to the brokenhearted
  And saves those who are crushed in spirit.

Psalm 34:17-18

Depression
NASB

2 Corinthians 4:8-10

We are afflicted in every way, but not crushed; perplexed, but not despairing; persecuted, but not forsaken; struck down, but not destroyed; always carrying about in the body the dying of Jesus, so that the life of Jesus also may be manifested in our body.

2 Corinthians 4:8-10

Sex
NASB

1 Thessalonians 4:3-5

This is the will of God, your sanctification; that is, that you abstain from sexual immorality; that each of you know how to possess his own vessel in sanctification and honor, not in lustful passion, like the Gentiles who do not know God.

1 Thessalonians 4:3-5

Sex
NASB

Matthew 5:27-28

You have heard that it was said, "You shall not commit adultery"; but I say to you that everyone who looks at a woman with lust for her has already committed adultery with her in his heart.

Matthew 5:27-28

Sex
NASB

1 Corinthians 6:18-20

Flee immorality. Every other sin that a man commits is outside the body, but the immoral man sins against his own body. Or do you not know that your body is a temple of the Holy Spirit who is in you, whom you have from God, and that you are not your own? For you have been bought with a price: therefore glorify God in your body.

1 Corinthians 6:18-20

Sex
NASB

Ephesians 5:3

Immorality or any impurity or greed must not even be named among you, as is proper among saints.

Ephesians 5:3

Sex
NASB

Romans 13:13-14

Let us behave properly as in the day, not in carousing and drunkenness, not in sexual promiscuity and sensuality, not in strife and jealousy. But put on the Lord Jesus Christ, and make no provision for the flesh in regard to its lusts.

Romans 13:13-14

Sex
NASB

Hebrews 13:4

Marriage is to be held in honor among all, and the marriage bed is to be undefiled; for fornicators and adulterers God will judge.

Hebrews 13:4

Money
NASB

Matthew 6:19-21

Do not store up for yourselves treasures on earth, where moth and rust destroy, and where thieves break in and steal. But store up for yourselves treasures in heaven, where neither moth nor rust destroys, and where thieves do not break in or steal; for where your treasure is, there your heart will be also.

Matthew 6:19-21

Money
NASB

Deuteronomy 8:17-18

You may say in your heart, "My power and the strength of my hand made me this wealth." But you shall remember the Lord your God, for it is He who is giving you power to make wealth.

Deuteronomy 8:17-18

Depression
KJV

2 Corinthians 4:8-10

We are troubled on every side, yet not distressed; we are perplexed, but not in despair; Persecuted, but not forsaken; cast down, but not destroyed; Always bearing about in the body the dying of the Lord Jesus, that the life also of Jesus might be made manifest in our body.

2 Corinthians 4:8-10

Depression
KJV

Psalm 34:17-18

The righteous cry, and the LORD heareth, and delivereth them out of all their troubles. The LORD is nigh unto them that are of a broken heart; and saveth such as be of a contrite spirit.

Psalm 34:17-18

Sex
KJV

Matthew 5:27-28

Ye have heard that it was said by them of old time, Thou shalt not commit adultery: But I say unto you, That whosoever looketh on a woman to lust after her hath committed adultery with her already in his heart.

Matthew 5:27-28

Sex
KJV

1 Thessalonians 4:3-5

This is the will of God, even your sanctification, that ye should abstain from fornication: That every one of you should know how to possess his vessel in sanctification and honour; Not in the lust of concupiscence, even as the Gentiles which know not God.

1 Thessalonians 4:3-5

Sex
KJV

Ephesians 5:3

Fornication, and all uncleanness, or covetousness, let it not be once named among you, as becometh saints.

Ephesians 5:3

Sex
KJV

1 Corinthians 6:18-20

Flee fornication. Every sin that a man doeth is without the body; but he that committeth fornication sinneth against his own body. What? know ye not that your body is the temple of the Holy Ghost which is in you, which ye have of God, and ye are not your own? For ye are bought with a price: therefore glorify God in your body, and in your spirit, which are God's.

1 Corinthians 6:18-20

Sex
KJV

Hebrews 13:4

Marriage is honourable in all, and the bed undefiled: but whoremongers and adulterers God will judge.

Hebrews 13:4

Sex
KJV

Romans 13:13-14

Let us walk honestly, as in the day; not in rioting and drunkenness, not in chambering and wantonness, not in strife and envying. But put ye on the Lord Jesus Christ, and make not provision for the flesh, to fulfil the lusts thereof.

Romans 13:13-14

Money
KJV

Deuteronomy 8:17-18

Thou say in thine heart, My power and the might of mine hand hath gotten me this wealth. But thou shalt remember the LORD thy God: for it is he that giveth thee power to get wealth.

Deuteronomy 8:17-18

Money
KJV

Matthew 6:19-21

Lay not up for yourselves treasures upon earth, where moth and rust doth corrupt, and where thieves break through and steal: But lay up for yourselves treasures in heaven, where neither moth nor rust doth corrupt, and where thieves do not break through nor steal: For where your treasure is, there will your heart be also.

Matthew 6:19-21

Depression
NIV

Psalm 34:17-18

The righteous cry out, and the LORD hears them;
  he delivers them from all their troubles.
The LORD is close to the brokenhearted
  and saves those who are crushed in spirit.

Psalm 34:17-18

Depression
NIV

2 Corinthians 4:8-10

We are hard pressed on every side, but not crushed; perplexed, but not in despair; persecuted, but not abandoned; struck down, but not destroyed. We always carry around in our body the death of Jesus, so that the life of Jesus may also be revealed in our body.

2 Corinthians 4:8-10

Sex
NIV

1 Thessalonians 4:3-5

It is God's will that you should be sanctified: that you should avoid sexual immorality; that each of you should learn to control his own body in a way that is holy and honorable, not in passionate lust like the heathen, who do not know God.

1 Thessalonians 4:3-5

Sex
NIV

Matthew 5:27-28

You have heard that it was said, "Do not commit adultery." But I tell you that anyone who looks at a woman lustfully has already committed adultery with her in his heart.

Matthew 5:27-28

Sex
NIV

1 Corinthians 6:18-20

Flee from sexual immorality. All other sins a man commits are outside his body, but he who sins sexually sins against his own body. Do you not know that your body is a temple of the Holy Spirit, who is in you, whom you have received from God? You are not your own; you were bought at a price. Therefore honor God with your body.

1 Corinthians 6:18-20

Sex
NIV

Ephesians 5:3

Among you there must not be even a hint of sexual immorality, or of any kind of impurity, or of greed, because these are improper for God's holy people.

Ephesians 5:3

Sex
NIV

Romans 13:13-14

Let us behave decently, as in the daytime, not in orgies and drunkenness, not in sexual immorality and debauchery, not in dissension and jealousy. Rather, clothe yourselves with the Lord Jesus Christ, and do not think about how to gratify the desires of the sinful nature.

Romans 13:13-14

Sex
NIV

Hebrews 13:4

Marriage should be honored by all, and the marriage bed kept pure, for God will judge the adulterer and all the sexually immoral.

Hebrews 13:4

Money
NIV

Matthew 6:19-21

Do not store up for yourselves treasures on earth, where moth and rust destroy, and where thieves break in and steal. But store up for yourselves treasures in heaven, where moth and rust do not destroy, and where thieves do not break in and steal. For where your treasure is, there your heart will be also.

Matthew 6:19-21

Money
NIV

Deuteronomy 8:17-18

You may say to yourself, "My power and the strength of my hands have produced this wealth for me." But remember the LORD your God, for it is he who gives you the ability to produce wealth.

Deuteronomy 8:17-18

Depression

2 Corinthians 4:8-10

We are pressed on every side by troubles, but we are not crushed. We are perplexed, but not driven to despair. We are hunted down, but never abandoned by God. We get knocked down, but we are not destroyed. Through suffering, our bodies continue to share in the death of Jesus so that the life of Jesus may also be seen in our bodies.

2 Corinthians 4:8-10

Depression

Psalm 34:17-18

The LORD hears his people when they call to
    him for help.
  He rescues them from all their troubles.
The LORD is close to the brokenhearted;
    he rescues those whose spirits are
      crushed.

Psalm 34:17-18

Sex

Matthew 5:27-28

You have heard the commandment that says, "You must not commit adultery." But I say, anyone who even looks at a woman with lust has already committed adultery with her in his heart.

Matthew 5:27-28

Sex

1 Thessalonians 4:3-5

God's will is for you to be holy, so stay away from all sexual sin. Then each of you will control his own body and live in holiness and honor—not in lustful passion like the pagans who do not know God and his ways.

1 Thessalonians 4:3-5

Sex

Ephesians 5:3

Let there be no sexual immorality, impurity, or greed among you. Such sins have no place among God's people.

Ephesians 5:3

Sex

1 Corinthians 6:18-20

Run from sexual sin! No other sin so clearly affects the body as this one does. For sexual immorality is a sin against your own body. Don't you realize that your body is the temple of the Holy Spirit, who lives in you and was given to you by God? You do not belong to yourself, for God bought you with a high price. So you must honor God with your body.

1 Corinthians 6:18-20

Sex

Hebrews 13:4

Give honor to marriage, and remain faithful to one another in marriage. God will surely judge people who are immoral and those who commit adultery.

Hebrews 13:4

Sex

Romans 13:13-14

Because we belong to the day, we must live decent lives for all to see. Don't participate in the darkness of wild parties and drunkenness, or in sexual promiscuity and immoral living, or in quarreling and jealousy. Instead, clothe yourself with the presence of the Lord Jesus Christ. And don't let yourself think about ways to indulge your evil desires.

Romans 13:13-14

Money

Deuteronomy 8:17-18

He did all this so you would never say to yourself, "I have achieved this wealth with my own strength and energy." Remember the LORD your God. He is the one who gives you power to be successful.

Deuteronomy 8:17-18

Money

Matthew 6:19-21

Don't store up treasures here on earth, where moths eat them and rust destroys them, and where thieves break in and steal. Store your treasures in heaven, where moths and rust cannot destroy, and thieves do not break in and steal. Wherever your treasure is, there the desires of your heart will also be.

Matthew 6:19-21

Depression ESV

Psalm 34:17-18

When the righteous cry for help, the LORD hears
  and delivers them out of all their troubles.
The LORD is near to the brokenhearted
  and saves the crushed in spirit.

Psalm 34:17-18

Depression ESV

2 Corinthians 4:8-10

We are afflicted in every way, but not crushed; perplexed, but not driven to despair; persecuted, but not forsaken; struck down, but not destroyed; always carrying in the body the death of Jesus, so that the life of Jesus may also be manifested in our bodies.

2 Corinthians 4:8-10

Sex ESV

1 Thessalonians 4:3-5

This is the will of God, your sanctification: that you abstain from sexual immorality; that each one of you know how to control his own body in holiness and honor, not in the passion of lust like the Gentiles who do not know God.

1 Thessalonians 4:3-5

Sex ESV

Matthew 5:27-28

You have heard that it was said, "You shall not commit adultery." But I say to you that everyone who looks at a woman with lustful intent has already committed adultery with her in his heart.

Matthew 5:27-28

Sex ESV

1 Corinthians 6:18-20

Flee from sexual immorality. Every other sin a person commits is outside the body, but the sexually immoral person sins against his own body. Or do you not know that your body is a temple of the Holy Spirit within you, whom you have from God? You are not your own, for you were bought with a price. So glorify God in your body.

1 Corinthians 6:18-20

Sex ESV

Ephesians 5:3

Sexual immorality and all impurity or covetousness must not even be named among you, as is proper among saints.

Ephesians 5:3

Sex ESV

Romans 13:13-14

Let us walk properly as in the daytime, not in orgies and drunkenness, not in sexual immorality and sensuality, not in quarreling and jealousy. But put on the Lord Jesus Christ, and make no provision for the flesh, to gratify its desires.

Romans 13:13-14

Sex ESV

Hebrews 13:4

Let marriage be held in honor among all, and let the marriage bed be undefiled, for God will judge the sexually immoral and adulterous.

Hebrews 13:4

Money ESV

Matthew 6:19-21

Do not lay up for yourselves treasures on earth, where moth and rust destroy and where thieves break in and steal, but lay up for yourselves treasures in heaven, where neither moth nor rust destroys and where thieves do not break in and steal. For where your treasure is, there your heart will be also.

Matthew 6:19-21

Money ESV

Deuteronomy 8:17-18

Beware lest you say in your heart, "My power and the might of my hand have gotten me this wealth." You shall remember the LORD your God, for it is he who gives you power to get wealth.

Deuteronomy 8:17-18

Money
NKJV

Philippians 4:11-13

I have learned in whatever state I am, to be content: I know how to be abased, and I know how to abound. Everywhere and in all things I have learned both to be full and to be hungry, both to abound and to suffer need. I can do all things through Christ who strengthens me.

Philippians 4:11-13

Money
NKJV

1 Timothy 6:9-10

Those who desire to be rich fall into temptation and a snare, and into many foolish and harmful lusts which drown men in destruction and perdition. For the love of money is a root of all kinds of evil, for which some have strayed from the faith in their greediness, and pierced themselves through with many sorrows.

1 Timothy 6:9-10

Money
NKJV

Matthew 6:24

No one can serve two masters; for either he will hate the one and love the other, or else he will be loyal to the one and despise the other. You cannot serve God and mammon.

Matthew 6:24

Money
NKJV

2 Corinthians 9:6-7

He who sows sparingly will also reap sparingly, and he who sows bountifully will also reap bountifully. So let each one give as he purposes in his heart, not grudgingly or of necessity; for God loves a cheerful giver.

2 Corinthians 9:6-7

Stress
NKJV

Matthew 11:28-30

Come to Me, all you who labor and are heavy laden, and I will give you rest. Take My yoke upon you and learn from Me, for I am gentle and lowly in heart, and you will find rest for your souls. For My yoke is easy and My burden is light.

Matthew 11:28-30

Stress
NKJV

Psalm 118:5-6

I called on the Lord in distress;
    The Lord answered me and set me in a
        broad place.
The Lord is on my side;
    I will not fear.
    What can man do to me?

Psalm 118:5-6

Stress
NKJV

Philippians 4:6-7

Be anxious for nothing, but in everything by prayer and supplication, with thanksgiving, let your requests be made known to God; and the peace of God, which surpasses all understanding, will guard your hearts and minds through Christ Jesus.

Philippians 4:6-7

Stress
NKJV

Psalm 73:26

My flesh and my heart fail;
    But God is the strength of my heart and my
        portion forever.

Psalm 73:26

Stress
NKJV

1 Peter 5:6-7

Therefore humble yourselves under the mighty hand of God, that He may exalt you in due time, casting all your care upon Him, for He cares for you.

1 Peter 5:6-7

Stress
NKJV

2 Corinthians 4:16-18

We do not lose heart. Even though our outward man is perishing, yet the inward man is being renewed day by day. For our light affliction, which is but for a moment, is working for us a far more exceeding and eternal weight of glory, while we do not look at the things which are seen, but at the things which are not seen. For the things which are seen are temporary, but the things which are not seen are eternal.

2 Corinthians 4:16-18

Money
NASB

1 Timothy 6:9-10

Those who want to get rich fall into temptation and a snare and many foolish and harmful desires which plunge men into ruin and destruction. For the love of money is a root of all sorts of evil, and some by longing for it have wandered away from the faith and pierced themselves with many griefs.

1 Timothy 6:9-10

Money
NASB

Philippians 4:11-13

I have learned to be content in whatever circumstances I am. I know how to get along with humble means, and I also know how to live in prosperity; in any and every circumstance I have learned the secret of being filled and going hungry, both of having abundance and suffering need. I can do all things through Him who strengthens me.

Philippians 4:11-13

Money
NASB

2 Corinthians 9:6-7

He who sows sparingly will also reap sparingly, and he who sows bountifully will also reap bountifully. Each one must do just as he has purposed in his heart, not grudgingly or under compulsion, for God loves a cheerful giver.

2 Corinthians 9:6-7

Money
NASB

Matthew 6:24

No one can serve two masters; for either he will hate the one and love the other, or he will be devoted to one and despise the other. You cannot serve God and wealth.

Matthew 6:24

Stress
NASB

Psalm 118:5-6

From my distress I called upon the LORD;
    The LORD answered me and set me in a
        large place.
The LORD is for me; I will not fear;
    What can man do to me?

Psalm 118:5-6

Stress
NASB

Matthew 11:28-30

Come to Me, all who are weary and heavy-laden, and I will give you rest. Take My yoke upon you and learn from Me, for I am gentle and humble in heart, and you will find rest for your souls. For My yoke is easy and My burden is light.

Matthew 11:28-30

Stress
NASB

Psalm 73:26

My flesh and my heart may fail,
    But God is the strength of my heart and my
        portion forever.

Psalm 73:26

Stress
NASB

Philippians 4:6-7

Be anxious for nothing, but in everything by prayer and supplication with thanksgiving let your requests be made known to God. And the peace of God, which surpasses all comprehension, will guard your hearts and your minds in Christ Jesus.

Philippians 4:6-7

Stress
NASB

2 Corinthians 4:16-18

We do not lose heart, but though our outer man is decaying, yet our inner man is being renewed day by day. For momentary, light affliction is producing for us an eternal weight of glory far beyond all comparison, while we look not at the things which are seen, but at the things which are not seen; for the things which are seen are temporal, but the things which are not seen are eternal.

2 Corinthians 4:16-18

Stress
NASB

1 Peter 5:6-7

Therefore humble yourselves under the mighty hand of God, that He may exalt you at the proper time, casting all your anxiety on Him, because He cares for you.

1 Peter 5:6-7

Money KJV

Philippians 4:11-13

I have learned, in whatsoever state I am, therewith to be content. I know both how to be abased, and I know how to abound: every where and in all things I am instructed both to be full and to be hungry, both to abound and to suffer need. I can do all things through Christ which strengtheneth me.

Philippians 4:11-13

Money KJV

1 Timothy 6:9-10

They that will be rich fall into temptation and a snare, and into many foolish and hurtful lusts, which drown men in destruction and perdition. For the love of money is the root of all evil: which while some coveted after, they have erred from the faith, and pierced themselves through with many sorrows.

1 Timothy 6:9-10

Money KJV

Matthew 6:24

No man can serve two masters: for either he will hate the one, and love the other; or else he will hold to the one, and despise the other. Ye cannot serve God and mammon.

Matthew 6:24

Money KJV

2 Corinthians 9:6-7

He which soweth sparingly shall reap also sparingly; and he which soweth bountifully shall reap also bountifully. Every man according as he purposeth in his heart, so let him give; not grudgingly, or of necessity: for God loveth a cheerful giver.

2 Corinthians 9:6-7

Stress KJV

Matthew 11:28-30

Come unto me, all ye that labour and are heavy laden, and I will give you rest. Take my yoke upon you, and learn of me; for I am meek and lowly in heart: and ye shall find rest unto your souls. For my yoke is easy, and my burden is light.

Matthew 11:28-30

Stress KJV

Psalm 118:5-6

I called upon the LORD in distress: the LORD answered me, and set me in a large place. The LORD is on my side; I will not fear: what can man do unto me?

Psalm 118:5-6

Stress KJV

Philippians 4:6-7

Be careful for nothing; but in every thing by prayer and supplication with thanksgiving let your requests be made known unto God. And the peace of God, which passeth all understanding, shall keep your hearts and minds through Christ Jesus.

Philippians 4:6-7

Stress KJV

Psalm 73:26

My flesh and my heart faileth: but God is the strength of my heart, and my portion for ever.

Psalm 73:26

Stress KJV

1 Peter 5:6-7

Humble yourselves therefore under the mighty hand of God, that he may exalt you in due time: Casting all your care upon him; for he careth for you.

1 Peter 5:6-7

Stress KJV

2 Corinthians 4:16-18

We faint not; but though our outward man perish, yet the inward man is renewed day by day. For our light affliction, which is but for a moment, worketh for us a far more exceeding and eternal weight of glory; While we look not at the things which are seen, but at the things which are not seen: for the things which are seen are temporal; but the things which are not seen are eternal.

2 Corinthians 4:16-18

Money NIV

1 Timothy 6:9-10

People who want to get rich fall into temptation and a trap and into many foolish and harmful desires that plunge men into ruin and destruction. For the love of money is a root of all kinds of evil. Some people, eager for money, have wandered from the faith and pierced themselves with many griefs.

1 Timothy 6:9-10

Money NIV

Philippians 4:11-13

I have learned to be content whatever the circumstances. I know what it is to be in need, and I know what it is to have plenty. I have learned the secret of being content in any and every situation, whether well fed or hungry, whether living in plenty or in want. I can do everything through him who gives me strength.

Philippians 4:11-13

Money NIV

2 Corinthians 9:6-7

Whoever sows sparingly will also reap sparingly, and whoever sows generously will also reap generously. Each man should give what he has decided in his heart to give, not reluctantly or under compulsion, for God loves a cheerful giver.

2 Corinthians 9:6-7

Money NIV

Matthew 6:24

No one can serve two masters. Either he will hate the one and love the other, or he will be devoted to the one and despise the other. You cannot serve both God and Money.

Matthew 6:24

Stress NIV

Psalm 118:5-6

In my anguish I cried to the LORD,
    and he answered by setting me free.
The LORD is with me; I will not be afraid.
    What can man do to me?

Psalm 118:5-6

Stress NIV

Matthew 11:28-30

Come to me, all you who are weary and burdened, and I will give you rest. Take my yoke upon you and learn from me, for I am gentle and humble in heart, and you will find rest for your souls. For my yoke is easy and my burden is light.

Matthew 11:28-30

Stress NIV

Psalm 73:26

My flesh and my heart may fail,
    but God is the strength of my heart
    and my portion forever.

Psalm 73:26

Stress NIV

Philippians 4:6-7

Do not be anxious about anything, but in everything, by prayer and petition, with thanksgiving, present your requests to God. And the peace of God, which transcends all understanding, will guard your hearts and your minds in Christ Jesus.

Philippians 4:6-7

Stress NIV

2 Corinthians 4:16-18

We do not lose heart. Though outwardly we are wasting away, yet inwardly we are being renewed day by day. For our light and momentary troubles are achieving for us an eternal glory that far outweighs them all. So we fix our eyes not on what is seen, but on what is unseen. For what is seen is temporary, but what is unseen is eternal.

2 Corinthians 4:16-18

Stress NIV

1 Peter 5:6-7

Humble yourselves, therefore, under God's mighty hand, that he may lift you up in due time. Cast all your anxiety on him because he cares for you.

1 Peter 5:6-7

Money
NLT

Philippians 4:11-13

I have learned how to be content with whatever I have. I know how to live on almost nothing or with everything. I have learned the secret of living in every situation, whether it is with a full stomach or empty, with plenty or little. For I can do everything through Christ, who gives me strength.

Philippians 4:11-13

Money
NLT

1 Timothy 6:9-10

People who long to be rich fall into temptation and are trapped by many foolish and harmful desires that plunge them into ruin and destruction. For the love of money is the root of all kinds of evil. And some people, craving money, have wandered from the true faith and pierced themselves with many sorrows.

1 Timothy 6:9-10

Money
NLT

Matthew 6:24

No one can serve two masters. For you will hate one and love the other; you will be devoted to one and despise the other. You cannot serve both God and money.

Matthew 6:24

Money
NLT

2 Corinthians 9:6-7

A farmer who plants only a few seeds will get a small crop. But the one who plants generously will get a generous crop. You must each decide in your heart how much to give. And don't give reluctantly or in response to pressure. "For God loves a person who gives cheerfully."

2 Corinthians 9:6-7

Stress
NLT

Matthew 11:28-30

Then Jesus said, "Come to me, all of you who are weary and carry heavy burdens, and I will give you rest. Take my yoke upon you. Let me teach you, because I am humble and gentle at heart, and you will find rest for your souls. For my yoke is easy to bear, and the burden I give you is light."

Matthew 11:28-30

Stress
NLT

Psalm 118:5-6

In my distress I prayed to the LORD,
    and the LORD answered me and set me free.
The LORD is for me, so I will have no fear.
    What can mere people do to me?

Psalm 118:5-6

Stress
NLT

Philippians 4:6-7

Don't worry about anything; instead, pray about everything. Tell God what you need, and thank him for all he has done. Then you will experience God's peace, which exceeds anything we can understand. His peace will guard your hearts and minds as you live in Christ Jesus.

Philippians 4:6-7

Stress
NLT

Psalm 73:26

My health may fail, and my spirit may grow
    weak,
    but God remains the strength of my heart;
    he is mine forever.

Psalm 73:26

Stress
NLT

1 Peter 5:6-7

So humble yourselves under the mighty power of God, and at the right time he will lift you up in honor. Give all your worries and cares to God, for he cares about you.

1 Peter 5:6-7

Stress
NLT

2 Corinthians 4:16-18

We never give up. Though our bodies are dying, our spirits are being renewed every day. For our present troubles are small and won't last very long. Yet they produce for us a glory that vastly outweighs them and will last forever! So we don't look at the troubles we can see now; rather, we fix our gaze on things that cannot be seen. For the things we see now will soon be gone, but the things we cannot see will last forever.

2 Corinthians 4:16-18

Money
ESV

1 Timothy 6:9-10

Those who desire to be rich fall into temptation, into a snare, into many senseless and harmful desires that plunge people into ruin and destruction. For the love of money is a root of all kinds of evils. It is through this craving that some have wandered away from the faith and pierced themselves with many pangs.

1 Timothy 6:9-10

Money
ESV

Philippians 4:11-13

I have learned in whatever situation I am to be content. I know how to be brought low, and I know how to abound. In any and every circumstance, I have learned the secret of facing plenty and hunger, abundance and need. I can do all things through him who strengthens me.

Philippians 4:11-13

Money
ESV

2 Corinthians 9:6-7

Whoever sows sparingly will also reap sparingly, and whoever sows bountifully will also reap bountifully. Each one must give as he has decided in his heart, not reluctantly or under compulsion, for God loves a cheerful giver.

2 Corinthians 9:6-7

Money
ESV

Matthew 6:24

No one can serve two masters, for either he will hate the one and love the other, or he will be devoted to the one and despise the other. You cannot serve God and money.

Matthew 6:24

Stress
ESV

Psalm 118:5-6

Out of my distress I called on the Lord;
 the Lord answered me and set me free.
The Lord is on my side; I will not fear.
 What can man do to me?

Psalm 118:5-6

Stress
ESV

Matthew 11:28-30

Come to me, all who labor and are heavy laden, and I will give you rest. Take my yoke upon you, and learn from me, for I am gentle and lowly in heart, and you will find rest for your souls. For my yoke is easy, and my burden is light.

Matthew 11:28-30

Stress
ESV

Psalm 73:26

My flesh and my heart may fail,
 but God is the strength of my heart and my
 portion forever.

Psalm 73:26

Stress
ESV

Philippians 4:6-7

Do not be anxious about anything, but in everything by prayer and supplication with thanksgiving let your requests be made known to God. And the peace of God, which surpasses all understanding, will guard your hearts and your minds in Christ Jesus.

Philippians 4:6-7

Stress
ESV

2 Corinthians 4:16-18

We do not lose heart. Though our outer self is wasting away, our inner self is being renewed day by day. For this light momentary affliction is preparing for us an eternal weight of glory beyond all comparison, as we look not to the things that are seen but to the things that are unseen. For the things that are seen are transient, but the things that are unseen are eternal.

2 Corinthians 4:16-18

Stress
ESV

1 Peter 5:6-7

Humble yourselves, therefore, under the mighty hand of God so that at the proper time he may exalt you, casting all your anxieties on him, because he cares for you.

1 Peter 5:6-7

Suffering

1 Peter 4:12-13

Do not think it strange concerning the fiery trial which is to try you, as though some strange thing happened to you; but rejoice to the extent that you partake of Christ's sufferings, that when His glory is revealed, you may also be glad with exceeding joy.

1 Peter 4:12-13

Suffering

NKJV

Romans 5:2-5

We . . . rejoice in hope of the glory of God. And not only that, but we also glory in tribulations, knowing that tribulation produces perseverance; and perseverance, character; and character, hope. Now hope does not disappoint, because the love of God has been poured out in our hearts by the Holy Spirit who was given to us.

Romans 5:2-5

Suffering

NKJV

2 Corinthians 1:3-4

Blessed be the God and Father of our Lord Jesus Christ, the Father of mercies and God of all comfort, who comforts us in all our tribulation, that we may be able to comfort those who are in any trouble, with the comfort with which we ourselves are comforted by God.

2 Corinthians 1:3-4

Suffering

NKJV

1 Peter 1:6-7

In this you greatly rejoice, though now for a little while, if need be, you have been grieved by various trials, that the genuineness of your faith, being much more precious than gold that perishes, though it is tested by fire, may be found to praise, honor, and glory at the revelation of Jesus Christ.

1 Peter 1:6-7

Suffering

NKJV

James 1:12

Blessed is the man who endures temptation; for when he has been approved, he will receive the crown of life which the Lord has promised to those who love Him.

James 1:12

Suffering

NKJV

James 1:2-4

My brethren, count it all joy when you fall into various trials, knowing that the testing of your faith produces patience. But let patience have its perfect work, that you may be perfect and complete, lacking nothing.

James 1:2-4

Love

NKJV

John 13:34-35

A new commandment I give to you, that you love one another; as I have loved you, that you also love one another. By this all will know that you are My disciples, if you have love for one another.

John 13:34-35

Love

NKJV

1 Corinthians 13:4-8

Love suffers long and is kind; love does not envy; love does not parade itself, is not puffed up; does not behave rudely, does not seek its own, is not provoked, thinks no evil; does not rejoice in iniquity, but rejoices in the truth; bears all things, believes all things, hopes all things, endures all things. Love never fails.

1 Corinthians 13:4-8

Love

NKJV

Romans 8:38-39

I am persuaded that neither death nor life, nor angels nor principalities nor powers, nor things present nor things to come, nor height nor depth, nor any other created thing, shall be able to separate us from the love of God which is in Christ Jesus our Lord.

Romans 8:38-39

Love

NKJV

1 John 4:20

If someone says, "I love God," and hates his brother, he is a liar; for he who does not love his brother whom he has seen, how can he love God whom he has not seen?

1 John 4:20

Suffering
NASB

Romans 5:2-5

We exult in hope of the glory of God. And not only this, but we also exult in our tribulations, knowing that tribulation brings about perseverance; and perseverance, proven character; and proven character, hope; and hope does not disappoint, because the love of God has been poured out within our hearts through the Holy Spirit who was given to us.

Romans 5:2-5

Suffering
NASB

1 Peter 4:12-13

Do not be surprised at the fiery ordeal among you, which comes upon you for your testing, as though some strange thing were happening to you; but to the degree that you share the sufferings of Christ, keep on rejoicing, so that also at the revelation of His glory you may rejoice with exultation.

1 Peter 4:12-13

Suffering
NASB

1 Peter 1:6-7

In this you greatly rejoice, even though now for a little while, if necessary, you have been distressed by various trials, so that the proof of your faith, being more precious than gold which is perishable, even though tested by fire, may be found to result in praise and glory and honor at the revelation of Jesus Christ.

1 Peter 1:6-7

Suffering
NASB

2 Corinthians 1:3-4

Blessed be the God and Father of our Lord Jesus Christ, the Father of mercies and God of all comfort, who comforts us in all our affliction so that we will be able to comfort those who are in any affliction with the comfort with which we ourselves are comforted by God.

2 Corinthians 1:3-4

Suffering
NASB

James 1:2-4

Consider it all joy, my brethren, when you encounter various trials, knowing that the testing of your faith produces endurance. And let endurance have its perfect result, so that you may be perfect and complete, lacking in nothing.

James 1:2-4

Suffering
NASB

James 1:12

Blessed is a man who perseveres under trial; for once he has been approved, he will receive the crown of life which the Lord has promised to those who love Him.

James 1:12

Love
NASB

1 Corinthians 13:4-8

Love is patient, love is kind and is not jealous; love does not brag and is not arrogant, does not act unbecomingly; it does not seek its own, is not provoked, does not take into account a wrong suffered, does not rejoice in unrighteousness, but rejoices with the truth; bears all things, believes all things, hopes all things, endures all things. Love never fails.

1 Corinthians 13:4-8

Love
NASB

John 13:34-35

A new commandment I give to you, that you love one another, even as I have loved you, that you also love one another. By this all men will know that you are My disciples, if you have love for one another.

John 13:34-35

Love
NASB

1 John 4:20

If someone says, "I love God," and hates his brother, he is a liar; for the one who does not love his brother whom he has seen, cannot love God whom he has not seen.

1 John 4:20

Love
NASB

Romans 8:38-39

I am convinced that neither death, nor life, nor angels, nor principalities, nor things present, nor things to come, nor powers, nor height, nor depth, nor any other created thing, will be able to separate us from the love of God, which is in Christ Jesus our Lord.

Romans 8:38-39

Suffering

1 Peter 4:12-13

Think it not strange concerning the fiery trial which is to try you, as though some strange thing happened unto you: But rejoice, inasmuch as ye are partakers of Christ's sufferings; that, when his glory shall be revealed, ye may be glad also with exceeding joy.

1 Peter 4:12-13

Suffering

Romans 5:2-5

We . . . rejoice in hope of the glory of God. And not only so, but we glory in tribulations also: knowing that tribulation worketh patience; and patience, experience; and experience, hope: And hope maketh not ashamed; because the love of God is shed abroad in our hearts by the Holy Ghost which is given unto us.

Romans 5:2-5

Suffering

2 Corinthians 1:3-4

Blessed be God, even the Father of our Lord Jesus Christ, the Father of mercies, and the God of all comfort; Who comforteth us in all our tribulation, that we may be able to comfort them which are in any trouble, by the comfort wherewith we ourselves are comforted of God.

2 Corinthians 1:3-4

Suffering

1 Peter 1:6-7

Wherein ye greatly rejoice, though now for a season, if need be, ye are in heaviness through manifold temptations: That the trial of your faith, being much more precious than of gold that perisheth, though it be tried with fire, might be found unto praise and honour and glory at the appearing of Jesus Christ.

1 Peter 1:6-7

Suffering

James 1:12

Blessed is the man that endureth temptation: for when he is tried, he shall receive the crown of life, which the Lord hath promised to them that love him.

James 1:12

Suffering

James 1:2-4

My brethren, count it all joy when ye fall into divers temptations; Knowing this, that the trying of your faith worketh patience. But let patience have her perfect work, that ye may be perfect and entire, wanting nothing.

James 1:2-4

Love

John 13:34-35

A new commandment I give unto you, That ye love one another; as I have loved you, that ye also love one another. By this shall all men know that ye are my disciples, if ye have love one to another.

John 13:34-35

Love

1 Corinthians 13:4-8

Charity suffereth long, and is kind; charity envieth not; charity vaunteth not itself, is not puffed up, Doth not behave itself unseemly, seeketh not her own, is not easily provoked, thinketh no evil; Rejoiceth not in iniquity, but rejoiceth in the truth; Beareth all things, believeth all things, hopeth all things, endureth all things. Charity never faileth.

1 Corinthians 13:4-8

Love

Romans 8:38-39

I am persuaded, that neither death, nor life, nor angels, nor principalities, nor powers, nor things present, nor things to come, Nor height, nor depth, nor any other creature, shall be able to separate us from the love of God, which is in Christ Jesus our Lord.

Romans 8:38-39

Love

1 John 4:20

If a man say, I love God, and hateth his brother, he is a liar: for he that loveth not his brother whom he hath seen, how can he love God whom he hath not seen?

1 John 4:20

Suffering
NIV

Romans 5:2-5

We rejoice in the hope of the glory of God. Not only so, but we also rejoice in our sufferings, because we know that suffering produces perseverance; perseverance, character; and character, hope. And hope does not disappoint us, because God has poured out his love into our hearts by the Holy Spirit, whom he has given us.

Romans 5:2-5

Suffering
NIV

1 Peter 4:12-13

Do not be surprised at the painful trial you are suffering, as though something strange were happening to you. But rejoice that you participate in the sufferings of Christ, so that you may be overjoyed when his glory is revealed.

1 Peter 4:12-13

Suffering
NIV

1 Peter 1:6-7

In this you greatly rejoice, though now for a little while you may have had to suffer grief in all kinds of trials. These have come so that your faith—of greater worth than gold, which perishes even though refined by fire—may be proved genuine and may result in praise, glory and honor when Jesus Christ is revealed.

1 Peter 1:6-7

Suffering
NIV

2 Corinthians 1:3-4

Praise be to the God and Father of our Lord Jesus Christ, the Father of compassion and the God of all comfort, who comforts us in all our troubles, so that we can comfort those in any trouble with the comfort we ourselves have received from God.

2 Corinthians 1:3-4

Suffering
NIV

James 1:2-4

Consider it pure joy, my brothers, whenever you face trials of many kinds, because you know that the testing of your faith develops perseverance. Perseverance must finish its work so that you may be mature and complete, not lacking anything.

James 1:2-4

Suffering
NIV

James 1:12

Blessed is the man who perseveres under trial, because when he has stood the test, he will receive the crown of life that God has promised to those who love him.

James 1:12

Love
NIV

1 Corinthians 13:4-8

Love is patient, love is kind. It does not envy, it does not boast, it is not proud. It is not rude, it is not self-seeking, it is not easily angered, it keeps no record of wrongs. Love does not delight in evil but rejoices with the truth. It always protects, always trusts, always hopes, always perseveres. Love never fails.

1 Corinthians 13:4-8

Love
NIV

John 13:34-35

A new command I give you: Love one another. As I have loved you, so you must love one another. By this all men will know that you are my disciples, if you love one another.

John 13:34-35

Love
NIV

1 John 4:20

If anyone says, "I love God," yet hates his brother, he is a liar. For anyone who does not love his brother, whom he has seen, cannot love God, whom he has not seen.

1 John 4:20

Love
NIV

Romans 8:38-39

I am convinced that neither death nor life, neither angels nor demons, neither the present nor the future, nor any powers, neither height nor depth, nor anything else in all creation, will be able to separate us from the love of God that is in Christ Jesus our Lord.

Romans 8:38-39

Suffering

1 Peter 4:12-13

Don't be surprised at the fiery trials you are going through, as if something strange were happening to you. Instead, be very glad—for these trials make you partners with Christ in his suffering, so that you will have the wonderful joy of seeing his glory when it is revealed to all the world.

1 Peter 4:12-13

Suffering
NLT

Romans 5:2-5

We confidently and joyfully look forward to sharing God's glory. We can rejoice, too, when we run into problems and trials, for we know that they help us develop endurance. And endurance develops strength of character, and character strengthens our confident hope of salvation. And this hope will not lead to disappointment. For we know how dearly God loves us, because he has given us the Holy Spirit to fill our hearts with his love.

Romans 5:2-5

Suffering
NLT

2 Corinthians 1:3-4

All praise to God, the Father of our Lord Jesus Christ. God is our merciful Father and the source of all comfort. He comforts us in all our troubles so that we can comfort others. When they are troubled, we will be able to give them the same comfort God has given us.

2 Corinthians 1:3-4

Suffering
NLT

1 Peter 1:6-7

So be truly glad. There is wonderful joy ahead, even though you have to endure many trials for a little while. These trials will show that your faith is genuine. It is being tested as fire tests and purifies gold—though your faith is far more precious than mere gold. So when your faith remains strong through many trials, it will bring you much praise and glory and honor on the day when Jesus Christ is revealed to the whole world.

1 Peter 1:6-7

Suffering
NLT

James 1:12

God blesses those who patiently endure testing and temptation. Afterward they will receive the crown of life that God has promised to those who love him.

James 1:12

Suffering
NLT

James 1:2-4

Dear brothers and sisters, when troubles come your way, consider it an opportunity for great joy. For you know that when your faith is tested, your endurance has a chance to grow. So let it grow, for when your endurance is fully developed, you will be perfect and complete, needing nothing.

James 1:2-4

Love
NLT

John 13:34-35

So now I am giving you a new commandment: Love each other. Just as I have loved you, you should love each other. Your love for one another will prove to the world that you are my disciples.

John 13:34-35

Love
NLT

1 Corinthians 13:4-8

Love is patient and kind. Love is not jealous or boastful or proud or rude. It does not demand its own way. It is not irritable, and it keeps no record of being wronged. It does not rejoice about injustice but rejoices whenever the truth wins out. Love never gives up, never loses faith, is always hopeful, and endures through every circumstance. . . . Love will last forever!

1 Corinthians 13:4-8

Love
NLT

Romans 8:38-39

I am convinced that nothing can ever separate us from God's love. Neither death nor life, neither angels nor demons, neither our fears for today nor our worries about tomorrow—not even the powers of hell can separate us from God's love. No power in the sky above or in the earth below—indeed, nothing in all creation will ever be able to separate us from the love of God that is revealed in Christ Jesus our Lord.

Romans 8:38-39

Love
NLT

1 John 4:20

If someone says, "I love God," but hates a Christian brother or sister, that person is a liar; for if we don't love people we can see, how can we love God, whom we cannot see?

1 John 4:20

Suffering ESV
Romans 5:2-5

We rejoice in hope of the glory of God. More than that, we rejoice in our sufferings, knowing that suffering produces endurance, and endurance produces character, and character produces hope, and hope does not put us to shame, because God's love has been poured into our hearts through the Holy Spirit who has been given to us.

Romans 5:2-5

Suffering ESV
1 Peter 4:12-13

Do not be surprised at the fiery trial when it comes upon you to test you, as though something strange were happening to you. But rejoice insofar as you share Christ's sufferings, that you may also rejoice and be glad when his glory is revealed.

1 Peter 4:12-13

Suffering ESV
1 Peter 1:6-7

In this you rejoice, though now for a little while, if necessary, you have been grieved by various trials, so that the tested genuineness of your faith—more precious than gold that perishes though it is tested by fire—may be found to result in praise and glory and honor at the revelation of Jesus Christ.

1 Peter 1:6-7

Suffering ESV
2 Corinthians 1:3-4

Blessed be the God and Father of our Lord Jesus Christ, the Father of mercies and God of all comfort, who comforts us in all our affliction, so that we may be able to comfort those who are in any affliction, with the comfort with which we ourselves are comforted by God.

2 Corinthians 1:3-4

Suffering ESV
James 1:2-4

Count it all joy, my brothers, when you meet trials of various kinds, for you know that the testing of your faith produces steadfastness. And let steadfastness have its full effect, that you may be perfect and complete, lacking in nothing.

James 1:2-4

Suffering ESV
James 1:12

Blessed is the man who remains steadfast under trial, for when he has stood the test he will receive the crown of life, which God has promised to those who love him.

James 1:12

Love ESV
1 Corinthians 13:4-8

Love is patient and kind; love does not envy or boast; it is not arrogant or rude. It does not insist on its own way; it is not irritable or resentful; it does not rejoice at wrongdoing, but rejoices with the truth. Love bears all things, believes all things, hopes all things, endures all things. Love never ends.

1 Corinthians 13:4-8

Love ESV
John 13:34-35

A new commandment I give to you, that you love one another: just as I have loved you, you also are to love one another. By this all people will know that you are my disciples, if you have love for one another.

John 13:34-35

Love ESV
1 John 4:20

If anyone says, "I love God," and hates his brother, he is a liar; for he who does not love his brother whom he has seen cannot love God whom he has not seen.

1 John 4:20

Love ESV
Romans 8:38-39

I am sure that neither death nor life, nor angels nor rulers, nor things present nor things to come, nor powers, nor height nor depth, nor anything else in all creation, will be able to separate us from the love of God in Christ Jesus our Lord.

Romans 8:38-39

Love
NKJV

1 Corinthians 13:1-3

Though I speak with the tongues of men and of angels, but have not love, I have become sounding brass or a clanging cymbal. And though I have the gift of prophecy, and understand all mysteries and all knowledge, and though I have all faith, so that I could remove mountains, but have not love, I am nothing. And though I bestow all my goods to feed the poor, and though I give my body to be burned, but have not love, it profits me nothing.

1 Corinthians 13:1-3

Love
NKJV

Matthew 22:37-40

"You shall love the Lord your God with all your heart, with all your soul, and with all your mind." This is the first and great commandment. And the second is like it: "You shall love your neighbor as yourself." On these two commandments hang all the Law and the Prophets.

Matthew 22:37-40

Love
KJV

1 Corinthians 13:1-3

Though I speak with the tongues of men and of angels, and have not charity, I am become as sounding brass, or a tinkling cymbal. And though I have the gift of prophecy, and understand all mysteries, and all knowledge; and though I have all faith, so that I could remove mountains, and have not charity, I am nothing. And though I bestow all my goods to feed the poor, and though I give my body to be burned, and have not charity, it profiteth me nothing.

1 Corinthians 13:1-3

Love
KJV

Matthew 22:37-40

Thou shalt love the Lord thy God with all thy heart, and with all thy soul, and with all thy mind. This is the first and great commandment. And the second is like unto it, Thou shalt love thy neighbour as thyself. On these two commandments hang all the law and the prophets.

Matthew 22:37-40

Love
NLT

1 Corinthians 13:1-3

If I could speak all the languages of earth and of angels, but didn't love others, I would only be a noisy gong or a clanging cymbal. If I had the gift of prophecy, and if I understood all of God's secret plans and possessed all knowledge, and if I had such faith that I could move mountains, but didn't love others, I would be nothing. If I gave everything I have to the poor and even sacrificed my body, I could boast about it; but if I didn't love others, I would have gained nothing.

1 Corinthians 13:1-3

Love
NLT

Matthew 22:37-40

"You must love the Lord your God with all your heart, all your soul, and all your mind." This is the first and greatest commandment. A second is equally important: "Love your neighbor as yourself." The entire law and all the demands of the prophets are based on these two commandments.

Matthew 22:37-40

Love
NASB

Matthew 22:37-40

"You shall love the Lord your God with all your heart, and with all your soul, and with all your mind." This is the great and foremost commandment. The second is like it, "You shall love your neighbor as yourself." On these two commandments depend the whole Law and the Prophets.

Matthew 22:37-40

Love
NASB

1 Corinthians 13:1-3

If I speak with the tongues of men and of angels, but do not have love, I have become a noisy gong or a clanging cymbal. If I have the gift of prophecy, and know all mysteries and all knowledge; and if I have all faith, so as to remove mountains, but do not have love, I am nothing. And If I give all my possessions to feed the poor, and if I surrender my body to be burned, but do not have love, it profits me nothing.

1 Corinthians 13:1-3

Love
NIV

Matthew 22:37-40

"Love the Lord your God with all your heart and with all your soul and with all your mind." This is the first and greatest commandment. And the second is like it: "Love your neighbor as yourself." All the Law and the Prophets hang on these two commandments.

Matthew 22:37-40

Love
NIV

1 Corinthians 13:1-3

If I speak in the tongues of men and of angels, but have not love, I am only a resounding gong or a clanging cymbal. If I have the gift of prophecy and can fathom all mysteries and all knowledge, and if I have a faith that can move mountains, but have not love, I am nothing. If I give all I possess to the poor and surrender my body to the flames, but have not love, I gain nothing.

1 Corinthians 13:1-3

Love
ESV

Matthew 22:37-40

You shall love the Lord your God with all your heart and with all your soul and with all your mind. This is the great and first commandment. And a second is like it: You shall love your neighbor as yourself. On these two commandments depend all the Law and the Prophets.

Matthew 22:37-40

Love
ESV

1 Corinthians 13:1-3

If I speak in the tongues of men and of angels, but have not love, I am a noisy gong or a clanging cymbal. And if I have prophetic powers, and understand all mysteries and all knowledge, and if I have all faith, so as to remove mountains, but have not love, I am nothing. If I give away all I have, and if I deliver up my body to be burned, but have not love, I gain nothing.

1 Corinthians 13:1-3